INSIGHT ⊙ GUIDES

EXPLORE

FIJI

PLAN & BOOK
YOUR TAILOR-MADE TRIP

BRAZIL

CHILE

ECUADOR

TAILOR-MADE TRIPS & UNIQUE EXPERIENCES CREATED BY LOCAL TRAVEL EXPERTS AT INSIGHTGUIDES.COM/HOLIDAYS

Insight Guides has been inspiring travellers with high-quality travel content for over 45 years. As well as our popular guidebooks, we now offer the opportunity to book tailor-made private trips completely personalised to your needs and interests.
By connecting with one of our local experts, you will directly benefit from their expertise and local know-how, helping you create memories that will last a lifetime.

HOW INSIGHTGUIDES.COM/HOLIDAYS WORKS

STEP 1

Pick your dream destination and submit an inquiry, or modify an existing itinerary if you prefer.

STEP 2

Fill in a short form, sharing details of your travel plans and preferences with a local expert.

STEP 3

Your local expert will create your personalised itinerary, which you can amend until you are completely satisfied.

STEP 4

Book securely online. Pack your bags and enjoy your holiday! Your local expert will be available to answer questions during your trip.

BENEFITS OF PLANNING & BOOKING AT
INSIGHTGUIDES.COM/HOLIDAYS

PLANNED BY LOCAL EXPERTS
The Insight Guides local experts are hand-picked, based on their experience in the travel industry and their impeccable standards of customer service.

SAVE TIME & MONEY
When a local expert plans your trip, you save time and money when you book, even during high season. You won't be charged for using a credit card either.

TAILOR-MADE TRIPS
Book with Insight Guides, and you will be in complete control of the planning process, from the initial selections to amending your final itinerary.

BOOK & TRAVEL STRESS-FREE
Enjoy stress-free travel when you use the Insight Guides secure online booking platform. All bookings come with a money-back guarantee.

WHAT OTHER TRAVELLERS THINK ABOUT TRIPS BOOKED AT INSIGHTGUIDES.COM/HOLIDAYS

Trip to Portugal

Every step of the planning process and the trip itself was effortless and exceptional. Our special interests, preferences and requests were accommodated resulting in a trip that exceeded our expectations.

Corinne, USA   ★★★★★

Trip to Vietnam

The organization was superb, the drivers professional, and accommodation quite comfortable. I was well taken care of! My thanks to your colleagues who helped make my trip to Vietnam such a great experience.

Heather   ★★★★★

919,611
Insight
2019

DON'T MISS OUT
BOOK NOW AT
INSIGHTGUIDES.COM/HOLIDAYS

CONTENTS

BEACH BUMS

Fiji is synonymous with sun-bleached white beaches, brushed by gently lapping waters. If this is your scene, head to the Blue Lagoon in the Yasawa Islands (route 9) and Natadola Beach (route 3).

RECOMMENDED ROUTES FOR...

FIJIAN CULTURE

Visiting a real Fijian village is an utterly unforgettable experience. The most authentic encounters can be enjoyed in the highland village of Navala (route 3) and in Namuamua on the Navua River (route 8).

ISLAND HOPPERS

There's no better cure for itchy feet than travelling around an archipelago of tropical islands, so get a multi-trip ferry ticket and begin bouncing around the Mamanuca (route 1) and Yasawa islands (route 9).

EXPLORERS

Independent travellers will relish getting away from the tourists and into the 'real' Fiji during 4x4 adventures in the Highlands (route 6) and during a visit to the less-visited islands of the country's north (route 10).

SCUBA DIVERS

Amazingly, Fiji is even more gorgeous below the water than it is above it. Dive into a kaleidoscope of coloured coral and fabulous fish in Fiji's north (route 10) or from the islands in the Yasawa group (route 9).

SURFERS

Wave riders will delight in the breaks served up by Malolo Barrier Reef in the Mamanuca Islands (route 1), and revel in the wonderful waves around Sigatoka (route 4) and Natadola Beach (route 3).

TROPICAL TRAIN SPOTTERS

You don't have to be a nerd to get a kick out of riding on the Coral Coast Railway (route 3) or to appreciate the sweet sight of the old sugar train wending through the palms in Lautoka (route 2).

URBANISTAS

Nobody visits Fiji looking for a gritty city, but Suva (route 5), the biggest metropolis in the South Pacific, delivers a taste of tropical town life. Contrast with the sleepy colonial feel of the country's old capital, Levuka (route 7).

INTRODUCTION

An introduction to Fiji's geography, customs and culture, plus illuminating background information on cuisine, history and what to do when you're there.

Welcome to Fiji!

EXPLORE FIJI

From the reefs that surround its many tropical islands, to the friendly villages and verdant heights of its highlands, there's so much more to explore in Fiji than just the first gorgeous beach you reach – although that's not a bad place to start.

For most people, mere mention of the word Fiji conjures up mental images of sun-soaked beaches, luxurious lagoon-based resorts, coral reefs scantily covered by a gentle gin-clear ocean, and tropical islands populated by welcoming and laidback locals, ever-ready with a smile and a cup of *yaqona*. And, true enough, you can find all of the above, but there's more to Fiji than *kava* and clichés.

Visitors often land in Nadi and immediately go seeking sun, sand, sea, snorkelling and surf in the archipelagos of Mananuca and Yasawa. For many, the Fiji experience is defined by the country's island culture, where time is an abstract concept, primarily measured by daylight hours and not marks on a clock, and everything that matters in life happens on the beach.

Yet Fiji is so much more than simply the sum of its islands. As somnambulant as it may sometimes seem, this is a modern country with a thriving economy and several vibrant multicultural urban centres, which offer the best restaurants in the region. The cultural mix that underpins 21st century Fiji is the subject of much internal debate, but for visitors, the country's ethnic diversity gives it a depth not seen elsewhere in Oceania, making it an even more sensational destination to explore.

GEOGRAPHY AND LAYOUT

Unless you're lucky enough to arrive on a yacht, your Fijian foray will almost certainly begin in Nadi, the country's main transport hub and home to the international airport. Nadi is on the west coast of Viti Levu, which at 4,000sq miles (10,360sq km), is by far the largest of the 332 islands that collectively comprise this gloriously scattered South Pacific nation, spread across more than 517,998sq km (200,000sq miles) of the South Pacific Ocean, between the latitudes 13° and 25° south and longitude 176° west and 177° east.

Nadi is the gateway to the hyper-popular islands of the Mamanuca Group (see page 38) and the slightly more remote Yasawa chain (see page 64). Every day, visitors, giddy with tropical excitement, are picked up by buses from hotels all around Nadi, to be taken to Denarau Island (connected to Viti Levu by a road bridge), where they board

The beach at Jean-Michel Cousteau Fiji Resort

various vessels and head off into the big blue of Bligh Water, to stay in beachside bures and play at being castaways for a week or two.

On the other side of Viti Levu is Suva, Fiji's capital and the largest city in Oceania – home to a large campus of the University of the South Pacific, myriad good restaurants and bars, and even a Central Business District. Linking Nadi and Suva, the Queens Road runs along the Coral Coast, a scenic stretch of seaside with the best beaches on the main island, which offers several interesting options for people looking to do daytrips. In the other direction from Nadi lies Fiji's second biggest city, the sugar-producing centre of Lautoka (see page 43).

Suva wasn't always the capital city – until 1877 that honour belonged to Levuka (see page 58), on the island of Ovalau, just east of Viti Levu. It's hard to imagine this sleepy place as a nation's capital, but the old colonial architecture and friendly feel of the town make it worth a visit.

Venture inland on Viti Levu – behind the wheel of a 4x4 vehicle, or by boat (see page 68) – and you can explore the wild green hinterland and highlands, where the populations of some villages still lead a very traditional existence. The main island is pretty mountainous, reaching 4,340ft (1,323m) at the peak of Mt Victoria.

Relatively few visitors fully explore Fiji's 'north' (see page 68) – a catch-all term describing Vanua Levu (2,137sq miles/5,535sq km) and Taveuni – the country's second and third biggest islands, respectively – plus the islands to the east and north of Viti Levu. Those that do discover some of the best scuba diving on the planet, and many other hidden treasures.

HISTORY

The first European to eyeball Fiji was the Dutch explorer Abel Tasman in 1643, but people have been living here for up to 4,000 years – the Lapita people being the islands' earliest known inhabitants. According to legend, the ancestors of today's Fijians arrived at Vuda Point near Viseisei Village (see page 42) led by the great chief Lutunasobasoba. Anthropologists, however, suggest the islands were initially settled by Austronesians and ocean-wandering explorers from Polynesia and Melanesia. Whatever went into the mix, the result was a proud people who scared the living daylights out of their neighbours, the Tongans, with their reputation as ferocious warriors and occasional cannibals. They called their land Viti, but the country's modern name originated from an Anglicisation of the Tongan word for the islands – Fisi – which Captain Cook, who sailed through in 1774, mispronounced as 'feejee'.

Captain Bligh floated through the Yasawa Islands in 1789, shortly after being jettisoned from the *Bounty* dur-

School children in the Lau Islands

ing the famous mutiny, and by the mid-19th century, a European settlement had been set up in Levuka to service the whaling ships that plied the South Pacific. By this time, British missionaries were visiting the islands too, in an (ultimately incredibly successful) attempt to convert the locals to Christianity. Fiji spent a spell as a semi-official independent kingdom under a militarily dominant chief called Ratu Sero Cakobau (aka Tui Vitu – the king of Fiji), but once the British had the islands properly in their sights it wasn't long before they were brought under the umbrella of the empire, and the Colony of Fiji was established in 1874. The islands remained a crown colony until 1970, when Fiji won independence as a Commonwealth realm, before a republic was declared in 1987, after a series of coups d'état.

CLIMATE

Fiji enjoys a tropical maritime climate. The summer season (November–April), when maximum temperatures average 30°C (86°F), is also known as the Wet, but it rains throughout the year. During the drier winter months (May–October), the maximum average temperature is 22°C (72 °F), but it gets much cooler in the highlands.

A cooling trade wind blows from the east-southeast for most of the year, crashing into the mountains of the principal islands, causing clouds to deposit rain. This is great for vegetation (which is almost luridly lush), but not for tourism. Consequently, most hotels and resorts are located on the western or 'dry' side of Viti Levu, many within close proximity to Nadi International Airport.

December to April is also cyclone season in the tropics. These severe events bring heavy rain and winds gusting up to and over 100 knots. Cyclones don't necessarily occur every year, but on average each decade will feature between 10 and 12.

POPULATION

Fiji has a population of just over 900,000 – about 70 percent of whom live on the main island of Viti Levu. Suva, the capital city, is home to 90,000. Besides indigenous Fijians, who have Melanesians and Polynesian ancestry and make up about 54 percent of the population, there's a large number of Indo-Fijian people. This group, which comprises around 40 percent of the country's permanent population, are descendants of Indian indentured labourers brought to Fiji by the British in the 19th century to work on the sugarcane plantations. Originally they were forbidden to purchase land or associate with the native Fijians, and as a result have retained much of the culture they brought with them from India. In recent decades there have been tensions between the cultures, especially seen during ugly inci-

Indo-Fijians in Sigatoka   *A rugby crowd in Suva*

dents around the coup of 2000, which was triggered by an election that made Mahendra Chaudhry the country's first Indo-Fijian Prime Minister – a stint that was short-lived. Most of the time, however, when differences are not being exploited by politicians, the communi-ties live side by side, even if there isn't a great degree of intermingling.

LOCAL CUSTOMS

Fijian people are famously friendly – to the point that it can be completely dis-

---

DON'T LEAVE FIJI WITHOUT...

Watching a local game of rugby. The real religion here is rugby. Watching a village game – or, even better, joining in with kids passing a ball around on the beach – is an unforgettable experience. Games erupt everywhere, but there are daily rugby sessions in Viseisei Village. See page 42.

Going to church. It's hard not to admire the pluck of 19th-century missionaries, who risked life and limb to spread the word around the South Pacific. And they did an extraordinary job – churches are packed on Sundays, with everyone wearing their best clothes. It's quite the spectacle – attend a beachside service in the Yasawa Islands for the prime view all round. See page 64.

Doing nothing on a beach for a day. Even Australians, who know a thing or two about decent beaches – rave about the quality of the sea and sandscape at peerless spots such as the Blue Lagoon. See page 66.

Leaving the coast behind to explore the highlands. As good as the beaches and islands are, they only present one of Fiji's faces – get behind the wheel of a 4-wheel drive and discover the spine of Viti Levu. See page 68.

Paddling a bamboo raft. Take a trip up the Navua River, visit a village, swim at the bottom of some waterfalls and have a bash at bilibili rafting. See page 61.

Chowing down on a *lovo*. You don't know the meaning of the word feast until you have tucked into a traditional *lovo* – a huge cornucopia of food, including various meats marinated in coconut cream and spices, and wrapped in leaves, all prepared in an underground earth oven. See page 16.

Trying *kava*. You probably won't be in Fiji for long before you come across a *kava* drinking session, a traditional ritual built around sharing a few bowls of *yaqona*, a mildly narcotic drink made from the root of a plant. Top spots to try this include the Yasawa Islands and inland villages on Viti Levu. See page 17.

Going diving. Incredibly, Fiji is even more beautiful below the water than it is above it, with thousands of soft corals and millions of fish creating a kaleidoscope of action at some of the world's best dive spots, particularly around the islands to the north of the country. See page 24.

arming – especially if you are travelling with children, who will be cuddled mercilessly, even by police and security staff. Friendliness is part of the culture, which regards visitors as honoured guests. Most people will smile, say hello and invite strangers into their homes and villages. If you are invited, it is courteous to reciprocate either by buying food, such as canned fish or corned beef, or 500g of yaqona (the powdered root of a plant used for ritual drinking). If you're staying at a resort, you'll almost certainly come across a yaqona *(kava)* ceremony at some point.

Be aware of cultural sensibilities – do not go to villages dressed in bikinis or brief shorts (speedos), as this will cause offence. You shouldn't wear a hat (even a cap) in such circumstances either, and never touch someone's head. Despite the overall courtesy and friendliness, it pays to be cautious. There are some who will take advantage of tourists, especially in market places.

RELIGION

A multi-racial, multi-cultural nation, Fiji is home to most of the world's major religions, as evidenced by the presence of Christian churches, Hindu temples and Muslim mosques in the towns and countryside. The majority of Fijians – some 64 percent – are Christian, with most being Methodist. Sunday is widely observed as a rest day, during which most shops will close and tours won't run. Visitors are often welcome to join Sunday worship.

Reflecting the size of the Indo-Fijian presence, nearly 28 percent of the population identify as Hindu.

POLITICS AND ECONOMICS

With several industries providing employment – including sugar production and tourism – and healthy reserves of forest, mineral, and fish resources, Fiji has a reasonably buoyant economy, one of the best developed and most resilient in the Pacific region. The political situation has been slightly less stable in recent decades, with a series of military coups – including a particularly complicated and dramatic one led by hardline nationalists in 2000, after Mahendra Chaudhry became the country's first Indo-Fijian Prime Minister.

The current Prime Minister is Commodore Frank Bainimarama, who originally seized power in a coup in 2006, but (after lots of shenanigans in the meantime) was democratically elected into office in September 2014, with his party winning 59 percent of the vote in an election that international observers deemed fair and credible. He won the November 2018 general election by a narrower margin with just over 50 percent of the vote.

LANGUAGE

English is the lingua franca, but schools also teach Fijian and Hindi. See page 100 for more.

Tourists enjoying the sunset, Viti Levu

TOP TIPS FOR VISITING FIJI

Bring your own good-quality mask and snorkel set. You will be wearing this gear a lot, and the mask is your window to the wonderful underwater world – so use something better than the cheap and cheerful equipment handed out by trip providers.

Go the extra mile and experience the real Fiji. Of course, it's all real, but when it comes to cultural traditions, what you see in a remote highland village like Navala inevitably feels less staged than what you might observe on an island teeming with tourists.

Go slip, slop, slap with the suncream, and wear a rash vest. Especially if you're snorkelling, when it is frighteningly easy to turn your back a lovely shade of lobster while you're distracted by the subaquatic action.

Pack some sand shoes alongside your flip-flops. The beaches aren't all made from squeaky-fine sand and sometimes you will need protection from rocks while you splash around. Sling in some walking boots while you're at it – then you're ready for anything.

Visit a local school. Many resorts offer guests the opportunity to do this – and the children love to see and chat to you. If you have children of your own, it can be a highly educational experience for them to see what conditions are like in schools elsewhere in the world.

Pack goodies. Bring a bucketload of sweets, lollies, pencils and pens to hand out to local children during village visits. It will absolutely make their day and happiness is highly infectious.

Water rules. Water is generally safe to drink in the bigger cities and plusher resorts and hotels (check), but always have a water purification solution to hand if you're travelling a bit further afield (there are enough plastic bottles in the world, you don't need to buy any more).

Village etiquette. It's customary to ask for the chief and to bring a present with you (*yaqona* is always a good option – it might seem strange, but think of it as though you're turning up at a friend's house with a bottle of wine).

Eat your own body weight in local food. It doesn't matter where you're from, you won't be harvesting *fruits de mer* like this again for a while. But be sure to get stuck into the Indo-Fijian curry scene too. Combine the two for a taste sensation.

Shop smart. When you're shopping for souvenirs, do your research and invest some time to find something made locally. Barter by all means, but pay a fair price for a proper piece of crafted work.

Go all-in. When looking in to accommodation, check whether there's an all-inclusive option covering meals and drinks as well. Depending on your habits, these can work out to be a good option.

Visit the local fresh-food markets. These places are full of colour and chaos, and make for some excellent people viewing.

Kokoda, served in a coconut

FOOD AND DRINK

With the enormous larder of the South Pacific at its disposal, it's no surprise that Fiji is famous for its sensational seafood, but the country's colourful cultural mix delivers a diverse range of fare, from traditional island feasts to spicy delights.

TRADITIONAL CUISINE

Fijian cuisine relies on fresh food, cooked simply, usually by boiling. Coconut cream, pressed from the shredded flesh of the nut, is either added during the cooking process or served as a sauce. When the cream is added during cooking, it is called *lolo*; when used as a sauce, it is known as *miti*.

Unsurprisingly, fish features prominently in the local diet, and if you're keen to try something classically Fijian, order *kokoda* – fresh, cubed fish marinated in lemon juice and coconut cream, typically served with hot chilli peppers.

Stew-style dishes are also very common, and standard ingredients that visitors may not have tasted before include dalo (the potato-like root of the taro plant), cassava (the root of the tapioca plant) and uvi (wild yam) – none of which are particularly strong tasting, but they all do a good job of filling you up with carbs. Breadfruit is also popular, but is only available seasonably.

Many Fijians are devout Christians and Sunday is always a feast day as in biblical times. This day is reserved for worship and family get-togethers around a midday feast, immediately after church. Even in villages where money is scarce, the number of dishes will be impressive: fresh fish, shellfish, seaweed and *heche de mer* (sea cucumber) from the lagoon, various root crops and vegetables, chicken and sometimes meat, and for dessert, cakes and puddings made from bananas and papayas, and fresh fruit. Often there will also be a Fijian version of chop suey and curry.

Lovos

The *lovo* is a Pacific Islands specialty, and an ingenious way of cooking large amounts of different food – a technique similar to a 'hangi' in New Zealand. First, a pit is dug and lined with river stones,

---

Food and drink prices

Throughout this guide we have used the following price ranges to denote the approximate cost of a two-course meal for one, with a drink.

$$$$ = above F$60
$$$ = F$40–60
$$ = F$20–$40
$ = F$20

Fresh seafood and chicken

A traditional lovo on Laucala Island

and then a fire is set, with more stones placed on top of pieces of wood. The size of the pit and of the stones will depend on the amount of food to be cooked – it may be as large as a small swimming pool, when a mountain of food can be cooked, including whole pigs, turtles, fish, beef, root crops and vegetables. The fire is allowed to die down and the unburned pieces and embers are removed and the stones leveled.

Green mid-ribs of coconut fronds are placed over the hot stones and food, traditionally wrapped in leaves (but foil is often used these days), is placed on the sticks, so that it doesn't come into direct contact with the stones. Banana leaves and sacking are used to cover the pit and soil is heaped over the *lovo* to trap the heat inside. A few hours later, the 'oven' is opened and the food is ready to be served. Most hotels and resorts feature *lovo* nights accompanied by Fijian entertainment – if you'd like to observe the cooking process, just ask nicely – most chefs will be delighted at your interest.

EATING OUT

Fiji's multicultural mix is well reflected on menus in restaurants and resorts all around the country. You will find a particularly broad range of eating options in the larger cities of Viti Levu, but the most widely available cuisines are ethnic Fijian (with high levels of coconut and carb content), Indian (with its emphasis on chillies and spices), Chinese (predom-

inantly Cantonese), European food (with a French bias) and traditional English.

DRINKS

A ubiquitous presence is Fiji Bitter served in ice-cold cans and stubbies (375ml bottles). Cocktails are popular too, but wine will be quite limited in most places, and relatively expensive. Soft drinks are widely available, including the local favourite: Pops Soda. Fiji's highland climate is good for farming coffee and cocoa.

Yaqona

It's virtually obligatory for every visitor to Fiji to experience a *yaqona* (*kava*) drinking session. This concoction – which is consumed across the islands of the South Pacific – is made from the ground root of the yaqona plant, mixed with water to form a slightly muddy looking liquid. The taste is unusual, slightly bitter but not nasty, and it produces a mildly narcotic effect, numbing the tongue slightly and producing a not-unpleasant feeling of contented sedation, conducive to *talanoa* (conversation). In a ceremony situation, it's usually accompanied by a chant, and sipped from coconut shells, and there are rules about the order participants drink it in. People of the Pacific have been downing this stuff for millennia, without serious side effects, but the drink is definitely a diuretic and it isn't recommended to mix kava with alcohol.

Colourful dresses in a Nadi shop

SHOPPING

If you find those funky Fijian dollars are burning a hole in your boardshorts, fear not, there are plenty of ways to get rid of them, in exchange for some seriously cool keepsakes of your visit.

Souvenir seekers and bargain hunters will not be disappointed with the shopping scene in Fiji. All of the larger towns have local markets, which are excellent for browsing when you're looking for something unique as a reminder of your trip, and the main cities also boast sizeable retail outlets and shopping strips where you can purchase beachwear and all sorts of essentials. There are a few top-end boutiques as well, and several places where you can pick up jewellery – both quirky (such as coconut husk bracelets, which are perennially popular with children) and classy (gold, silver and gems) – at very reasonable rates.

Food markets are always lively and colourful – full of the aromas and tastes of the tropics – with stalls overflowing with fresh fruits and various vegetables that aren't commonly seen in supermarkets at home. Municipal markets offer the best opportunity for absorbing the local scene. You can stand to one side with a slice of fresh pineapple or melon in hand, and indulge in some fascinating people watching without feeling that you're intruding.

Don't forget to take your camera along to capture these vibrant scenes. If you don't own one, the trade in duty free electronic goods is pretty brisk in Fiji, and you might be able to pick up a watch or camera for a good price.

There are many bargains to be found, especially for those with sharp bartering skills, but save your holiday haggling for the occasions when you're shopping in markets, where it's expected – private shopkeepers and boutique owners don't appreciate attempts to squeeze their prices quite so much.

SOUVENIRS

Great potential mementos of your time in Fiji include carved bowls, woven fabrics, tap cloth, sarongs, artworks, clothes (including hand-painted T-shirts), and handmade items such as coconut soap and jewellery.

For a really top-quality keepsake, you might want to hunt down some of Fiji's famous black pearls.

Handicrafts

As usual, when buying locally crafted items, you get what you pay for – trad-

Mask at Jack's Handicrafts   *Stall selling seashells and necklaces*

ers will not part with genuinely hand-made products for knockdown prices. And the choice is formidable. Handicrafts and artefacts include well-made replicas of old weapons, wooden bowls used for ritual purposes and for serving *yaqona* (see page 17), mats, fans and baskets woven out of pandanus, pottery and *masi* (also known as *tapa*, a type of bark cloth).

Note: it's illegal to take *tabua* (sperm whale teeth, which are of great ritual value in Fiji) out of the country. It's also worth considering how other souvenirs, such as exotic sea shells, have been sourced – there are complex ethical issues around this, but nothing made from skin, shell, bone, feather or fur comes with a completely clean conscience, and some products won't get past your home-country custom officials either. Buying anything made from coral is particularly objectionable.

Amid all of the treasure and trash that you might chance across in Fiji's municipal markets and in the heart of handicraft shops, often right next to the tanoa (kava bowls) and masi (tapa cloth), you'll almost certainly see some strange four-pronged wooden forks for sale. These intriguing investments are one of the more macabre souvenirs you are ever likely to buy, because they are cannibal forks – styled in the fashion of the traditional instruments used to eat human flesh on these very islands, just a few centuries ago (see box).They certainly make an interesting pres-

Fiji's cannibals

One aspect of Fiji's past that never fails to fascinate and horrify visitors, is the tradition of cannibalism once widely practised in the islands. Although it's commonly accepted that it did happen, the details are more debatable. Some theories suggest the practice increased after the arrival of Europeans (which did up the ante in tribal turf wars, with the introduction of modern weaponry), but most sources agree that cannibalism had been going on for centuries before contact was made – since 400BC according to the Fiji Museum. There are various theories about why cannibalism was practiced – some claim it originated from a simple need to eat during times of famine, but most argue the act was as much about symbolism as it was about sustenance. Certainly the bodies of enemies were commonly consumed, often with some ceremony. Human flesh, *bokola*, was usually reserved for notables, and was eaten with a special fork (sometimes made from a human leg bone), replicas of which you can now buy today as a souvenir. The most famous victim to go into a pot was Reverend Baker, an English missionary whose sorry tale is the subject of Jack London's short story *The Whale Tooth*. A particularly infamous Fijian cannibal was a hungry character called Udre Udre, who lived in Rakiraki during the 1800s and is believed to have eaten between 872 and 999 people.

Suva's fruit and vegetable market

ent for people back home, especially if you don't tell them the backstory until they're using them to serve the salad.

Clothing

In markets and shops across the country you'll find a very good selection of hand-dyed muslin cotton *sulus* – the Fijian name for wraparound sarongs known throughout the Pacific by various names, including *lava lava* and *pareo*.

There are dozens of clothing stores, with an excellent selection of T-shirts and casual wear. Fiji is a major exporter of clothing to Australia, New Zealand and the United States. Prices are low in comparison to these countries, even for some of the better-quality clothes.

And, of course, you can't leave Fiji without a few fabulous floral shirts in your suitcase. A range of locally made clothes – including some cacophonous shirts and brightly patterned blouses – can be found in Jacks of Fiji (www.jacksfiji.com), which has stores in Nadi, Nausori, Suva (MHCC shopping centre), Sigatoka, Lautoka, Labasa and Ba.

SHOPPING AREAS

Each town has a municipal market, which typically opens early in the morning and closes at 5pm. Predictably, Suva has the largest. These are always colourful and chaotic affairs, but they're especially so on Friday and Saturday mornings, when the markets are at their busiest, with vendors spilling onto the footpaths and even the roads. Fresh vegetables, root crops, seasonal fruit such as avocado, pineapple, mango, papaya and banana, spices essential for Indian cuisine, piles of dried *yaqona* and local tobacco cured into coils are usually on display.

Suva

For artefacts, fabrics and *ibis* (mats), the Suva Curio Handicraft Centre (see page 53) is a good market at which to browse and barter for souvenirs. Be a bit careful about what you buy – not everything is quite as kosher and individually handcrafted as the stallholders might claim – but bargains and keepsakes can certainly be found among all the treasure and the trash. Cumming Street is another hotspot for scoring a deal on anything from new threads to handicrafts, via a whole range of electronic gear.

Downtown Suva also boasts several boutiques that will be of interest for those at the cutting edge of the sartorial scene, such as the Treehouse Boutique (Damodar City shopping centre) a very cool specialist store for women, where traditional fabrics and prints are available in trendy cuts, alongside unique bags and jewellery.

Nadi and Denarau

Fiji's transport hub of Nadi has a cracking produce market, where you can pick up all manner of colourful tropical fruits and other fresh grub. There aren't

Shoppers in Suva

many souvenirs as such, but you've got a good chance of getting some fantastic photographs. Brave Main Street for a bout of rough and ready roadside shopping, where touts will vigorously compete for your attention (and dollars).

For a study in contrast, head to Port Denarau Retail Centre, where a more mainstream and clinical atmosphere prevails (this is a good place to pick up any essentials such as sun cream and toiletries that you may need).

Sigatoka

On the Queens Road between Nadi and Suva, just east of Sigatoka in the settlement of Korotogo, you'll find Hot Glass Fiji (www.hotglassfiji.com), the country's first glass-blowing studio, where pieces inspired by the natural landscape make the perfect reminder of your visit.

Levuka

There's a handicraft market in the old capital of Levuka, and the main (only) thoroughfare of Beach Street has several second-hand clothes stores featuring famous Australian brands at bargain prices.

Vanua Levu

Savusavu Bay is the place to pick up Fijian black pearls. These prized jewels, produced by black-lipped oysters, are farmed in the waters of the bay, and Savusavu is home to J Hunter Pearls (www.fijipearls.com). Always inspect pearls closely for quality.

Shopping tips

Strolling down the streets of Nadi, Lautoka or Suva is fun. The air is usually heavy with the smell of incense, the aroma of spicy foods and loud sounds of Hindi music. Sometimes, however, the shopkeepers can be a little over enthusiastic with their 'g'day mate!' greetings, and their tenacious efforts to try and get customers into their stores. Most visitors take it in their stride, but some find the touts annoying. Even if this attention doesn't bother you, do beware of the so-called 'sword sellers.' Fiji is such a genuinely friendly place that many visitors to Suva, Nadi and Lautoka – especially travellers who have already spent time in the islands – fall easy prey to the 'sword sellers'. Their ploy is simple: a 'sword seller' will first make friends with a cheery 'bula!' or 'hello, mate!' and then proceed with inquiries about your family and country of origin. He will ask your name, while simultaneously fishing out a sword-shaped piece of wood. Before you know it, your name will be carved onto the sword, and demands will be made for payment. If you find yourself in this situation, simply walk away. Just keep walking and do not look back. If necessary, walk into the nearest store and ask the shopkeeper to call the police. Beware also of 'guides' who promise to take you to shops where you will get the 'best' bargains.

A meke at the Jean-Michel Cousteau Fiji Resort

ENTERTAINMENT

For many visitors, Fiji is all about kicking back with a cocktail on the beach, but there are other entertainment options to explore in paradise.

Fiji is a small country with a scattered population and little in the way of large cities, so visitors will need to manage their entertainment expectations accordingly – there is no national orchestra, no ballet and no theatre, and the nightlife options are somewhat limited.

That said, there is plenty of local culture to enjoy; hotels, resorts and lodges invariably stage a range of shows and activities to keep guests amused in the evenings (from traditional dancing to hermit crab racing and coconut bowling); and in the cities you will find bars and the occasional club where an eclectic mix of locals, ex-pats, sailors and visitors go to let their hair down and shake their thing.

TRADITIONAL DANCE

Whether you're staying in a resort or visiting a village, you may very well be welcomed with a *meke* – a dance, traditionally performed either by groups of men, or groups of women. These days a *meke* can take many forms, with touristy resorts hamming them up to the max.

To see more extensive dance performances – which often tell a narrative taken from Fijian legend – check out the Oceania Centre for Arts & Culture in Suva, part of the University of the South Pacific (www.usp.ac.fj; see page 52), where theatre groups and dance troupes put on shows.

BARS AND NIGHTLIFE

Most large hotels have resident bands and discos, where you'll meet a lot of tourists, but there are plenty of places where you can party on with the locals. Some nightclubs in Fiji will continue bouncing until the early hours of the morning, or as long as there is a large crowd present, although technically, on Saturday nights they are supposed to close at the stroke of midnight because of the Sunday Observance Decree. Like most places in the world, things can get a little feisty at some of the local late-night haunts, so it's best to keep your wits about you.

Suva
Unsurprisingly, Suva has Fiji's most active entertainment scene, particularly around

Classic Fijian entertainment: rugby sevens against New Zealand

the corner of MacArthur Street and Victoria Parade, where pub/club O'Reilly's has long been a draw for pool shooters, beer hounds and night owls. Other clubs in the area include Onyx, which has a dancefloor and a lounge area, and pumps out party tunes into the wee hours. Further south on Victoria Parade, Traps Bar is another popular watering hole, with a sports-orientated bar and a main bar, plus live music at least once a week. The major hotels, such as the Holiday Inn, also have bars that are fine for casual drinks during the day.

Nadi and Denarau
In Nadi, you can check out the Ice Bar on Queens Road for all sorts of late night shenanigans, or try the Nadi Farmer's Club on Ashram Road, where a lovely riverside setting creates the perfect spot for a sunny afternoon of beer sipping, after which you can often enjoy fire dancing performances and live music. In nearby Denarau, the classy Rhum-Ba (in Denarau Yacht Club) is a chic place to sink a few rums.

Vanua Levu
Over on Vanua Levu, Savusavu has a Yacht Club, which is a pleasant bar to down a few waterside drinks among a crowd of yachties and ex-pats - once you've become a temporary member. The Planters' Club also lets non-members in, and has a Sunday *lovo* (traditionally cooked feast, see page 16) once a month. But if you'd rather get jiggy with it, mooch along to Uro's – this club's name means sexy, and it features a young crowd dancing to international music over the weekend.

CINEMA

Suva has a couple of modern multiplex cinemas: Damodar City on Grantham Road and Village 6 on Scott St. Lautoka has the Village 4 Cinemas on Namoli Avenue. All of which show a mixture of Bollywood and Hollywood flicks.

SPORT

Rugby is the sport of choice right across Fiji. Watching a local game in the countryside is a fantastic experience, but if you want to see the really big boys playing, keep an eye out for fixtures being played at the ANZ National Stadium in Suva, which is located near the university, and hosts both league and union games at international level, plus football (soccer) matches.

For a spectator sport of a very different nature, check out a game of golf at one of Fiji's five premier courses – The Pearl at Rovodrau Bay, Denarau Golf Club near Nadi, the Fiji Club in Suva, Natadola Bay Club and the Nadi Airport Club – where professionals show how it's done during top-level tournaments including the Fiji International. If home-grown hero Vijay Singh is in town, expect excitement levels to be at fever pitch. See page 26 for information about playing golf.

Kayaking over crystal-clear waters

ACTIVITIES

For those looking for an active holiday, Fiji offers a vast array of aquatic adventures to dive into, from scuba diving to stand-up paddleboarding, while there's plenty of trail action on the bigger islands for hikers and bikers too.

Fiji isn't all about beach bumming – plenty of active people come here to experience outdoor sports in a glorious tropical environment. The scuba diving is world-class, but there are many other adventure pursuits to try your hand at too, including mountain biking, hiking, kayaking and SUP.

SCUBA DIVING AND SNORKELLING

There are more dive sites in Fiji than you could possibly explore in a whole lifetime. They're all exceptional, but some spots – such as the Somosomo Strait, which runs between Taveuni Island and Vanua Levu – deserve special mention. The strait earned Fiji bragging rights as the 'Soft Coral Capital of the World', and sites such as the Zoo, Rainbow Reef and the Great White Wall make regular appearances in experts' lists of 'Top 10 Dive Locations in the World'.

Dozens of dive companies offer one- or two-tank dives, and most also deliver diving instruction for people who want to become certified bubble blowers. Serious divers might consider getting a berth on a live-aboard boat. Recommended operators include Scuba Bula (tel: 628 0190; www.scubabula.com) and Reef Safari (tel: 675 0566; www.reefsafari.com/fiji), who operate via major hotels, from the Yasawas to Wananavu.

Based at the Lagoon Resort in Pacific Harbour, Beqa Adventure Divers (www.fijisharkdive.com) offer one of the best shark dives on the planet, during which you can swim with up to eight species of shark – including bull sharks and even the occasional tiger – with no cage.

The best time to dive in Fiji is during the dry season, from May to October, when water visibility often exceeds 30 metres (98 ft). And if you don't dive, and don't want to learn, the snorkelling in places such as the Yasawa Islands is free and almost as mind blowing. Plus, there's no time limit on it. Many of the dive operators run island hopping snorkelling tours as well.

FISHING

Fishing in Fiji spans deep-sea sport fishing (for marlin, sailfish, yellowfin,

Scuba diving

SUP off Castaway Island

dog-tooth tuna, shark, wahoo, giant trevally and mahi-mahi), shore fishing (for tropical trevallys, barracuda, queenfish, coral trout and Spanish mackerel), family friendly lagoon fishing, fly fishing (for wily bonefish on tidal flats) and river fishing (for large mouth bass).

Most resort hotels include game fishing as part of the optional activities available to guests. Some of the resorts own and operate their own fishing boats; others operate boats in association with subcontracting companies. Fiji's wahoo average 25kg (55lb), but fish twice that weight are also caught. Walu (Spanish mackerel and a close cousin to the wahoo) are also plentiful from August to February.

PADDLING

Whitewater paddling is enormously popular in Fiji, with companies such as Rivers Fiji (tel: 345 0147; www.riversfiji.com) running trips along Upper Navua Gorge, Middle Navua River and Wainikoroiluva (Luva) River. Paddlers, on rafts (on the Upper Navua) and inflatable kayaks (on the Middle Navua and Luva), thread through rainforest-fringed valleys, negotiating rock mazes and rapids that range from class II to class III, depending on conditions. You can do single-day experiences, or build your whole trip around an epic adventure such as the 8-day Highlands to Islands Ultimate

Fiji Explorer, which sees participants rafting, sea kayaking and snorkelling, before they get to do any relaxing in resorts. Trips generally incorporate lunch, and sometimes a village visit. Look out for traditional *bilibili* (bamboo canoe) races, and if you get a chance to have a go on one of these pole- and/or paddle-propelled craft – give it a go.

SURFING AND SUP

Fiji has some sensational surfing spots, from learner waves through to the famously super-challenging Cloudbreak off Viti Levu. Other popular breaks include Restaurants, aka 'Cloudbreak's Little Brother'; Sigatoka River mouth; Natadola Beach; the fantastically reliable Frigate Passage; Beqa Island; Yanuca Island; Tavarua and Namotu.

The best surfing season is in the dry winter months from May to October, when huge breaks are caused by the low pressure system. Fiji's lagoons and many reef-protected beaches are also perfect for stand-up paddleboarding (SUP), one of the most popular sports to emerge in recent years.

HIKING

There are walking trails all over Fiji, including in Koroyanitu National Park and Colo-i-Suva Forest Park on Viti Levu, and Bouma National Park on

Jungle trek on Taveuni

Taveuni, which you can trek independently (take plenty of water, and don't underestimate how challenging the terrain can be), or hike with a company like Talanoa Treks (tel: 998 0560; www.talanoa-treks-fiji.com), who organise walks to places including Nabalasere waterfalls and Wailotua Caves.

BIKING

The islands' tracks are great for those who like to explore on two wheels too. Stinger Bicycles (tel: 992 2301; www.stingerbikes.com), based in Nadi, offer mountain bike rental plus guided tours around various ace Viti Levu trails. The rental bikes are good quality (Avanti/Gary Fisher), and come with helmet, tools and a spare inner tube. Guided tours cater for beginners through to experienced riders, and include options such as a ride into the Nausori Highlands, and a 25km (15.5 miles) loop around the 'Magic Mountains'.

GOLF

The combination of Fiji's tropical climate, laid-back no-rush atmosphere, abundant hotels and resorts, and epic natural surrounds make the islands perfect for golf, and the country delivers in spades, with a range of golf courses offering top-quality greens, fairways and facilities for all levels of player, from the fair-weather weekend hacker to the handicap endowed serious amateur and even seasoned professionals. Fiji actually boasts some world-class golf courses, and it's not at all unusual to see lines of expensive-looking bags full of clubs coming off the airport carousel amid everyone else's luggage.

There are more than a dozen 9-hole courses spread across the islands – including those in Ba, Labasa, Lautoka, Rakiraki, Nadi, Naviti, Taveuni, and Yanuca – and five world-class 18-hole championship capable courses: Denarau Golf and Racquet Club, Nadi Airport Golf Club, Natadola Bay Championship Golf Course, Pacific Harbour Golf & Country Club, and Fiji Golf Club in Suva. Of the bigger courses, Denarau is possibly the pick of the bunch, and is certainly one of the most challenging. With water hazards on 15 of its 18 holes, this is a par 72 course spread across 7,200 yards/metres, punctuated by palm trees and tidal waterways. The signature hole is the 173-yard 17th, which carries over water (as do the other par 4 holes).

The Pearl South Pacific Fiji Resort was one of the first venues to jump on the lucrative golf cart, building a course designed by American Architects Gary Roger Baird and Robert Trent Jones Jr in 1977, in time to host the World Amateur Championships the following year. It remains at the

Shangri-La's Fijian Resort golf course

top of its game, and one of the most iconic holes is the 6th — a par 5 that rumbles right through the jungle.

Golf has granted prominence (and immense wealth) to Vijay Singh — probably the most famous Fijian in the entire world, who was involved in the design and layout of the fairways at the Natadola Bay course, until a bust-up with the developers led to the one-time World Number One walking away. It's still a fantastic course, though, with challenges including an epic 544-yard 6th, and several par 4 holes.

If there was any residual bad blood, it didn't stop Singh from taking part in the Fiji International (www.fijiinternational.com), which, in 2014, became Fiji's first ever internationally broadcast golf tournament. The annual event takes place in varying months and is an important fixture on the Asian Tour. It has drawn in top-ranking players from Australia, Belgium, Canada, China, Fiji, Germany, India, New Zealand, South Africa, Thailand and the United States in the past. The action means images of the country are beamed into an estimated 400 million homes around the globe. Vijay Singh returned for the 2018 Fiji International, making it his fifth year in a row at the competition. It was won by Gaganjeet Bhullar of India with Singh coming 25th. Fiji International 2019 will be held at the Natadola Bay Championship Golf Course.

Vijay Singh

The son of an airplane technician, Vijay Singh is an Indo-Fijian who was born in Lautoka, but grew up in Nadi, where the family were apparently too poor to be able to afford golf balls and practised their swing on coconuts instead. After playing several sports including snooker, cricket, football and rugby, he settled on golf and turned professional in 1982. A towering presence on the course — he's nicknamed the Big Fijian — and a natural talent, he won the Malaysian PGA Championship just two years later. His career wobbled after accusations that he had doctored his score card, which resulted in his expulsion from the Asian Tour in 1985, but by the end of the 1980s this was well behind him and he won his first PGA Tour event in 1993. Singh's prize-winning tally for the year 2003, when he turned 40, was over US$7.5 million (more than Tiger Woods), and in September the following year he overtook Woods at the top of the Official World Golf Ranking with victory at the Deutsche Bank Championship in Massachusetts, ending Tiger's 264-week streak as king of the golf world. Singh was inducted into the Hall of Fame in October 2006, aged 43, the youngest ever electee. Although his game is now in decline, he has topped US$60 million in PGA Tour career earnings.

The paint flies at Holi

FESTIVALS

Fiji's festivals and public holidays reflect the multicultural nature of the country's population, with dates from various calendars and cultures recognised, observed and celebrated.

Every day feels like a holiday when you're on the beach in Fiji, and in the past the country certainly did like to find an excuse to celebrate as often as possible – with public holidays for all sorts of things. Until the early 1990s, Fiji even observed Prince Charles' birthday, 15 November, with a national holiday – the only country in the Commonwealth to do so.

Fiji celebrated Queen Elizabeth II's official birthday – on 15 June – until even more recently, but in 2012 that too was abolished. However there remain some monarchists who celebrate it privately. Queen Elizabeth II was ditched as Fiji's head of state in 1987, after the country became a republic. This is partly because the chiefs still recognise her as the Tui Viti, or Paramount Chief of Fiji. Since the series of coups in the 1990s, however, the military-dominated governments have been a bit stingier, and several other national holidays have been binned.

Fiji lacks its own ancient festivals and carnivals. Events which may have been celebrated by Fijians before the introduction of Christianity no longer exist, and all the dates on the calendar are imports from other cultures and parts of the world. These include all the major Christian festivals, such as Easter and Christmas, which are observed with accompanying holidays; the Hindu festival of Diwali (Festival of Lights); and the end of the Muslim fasting month of Ramadan.

Other festivals such as the Hibiscus Festival in Suva in August, the Sugar Festival in Lautoka in September, and the Bula Festival in Nadi in July are of relatively recent origin, but are becoming part of the fabric of Fiji. As dates vary from year to year, it's best to check with Fiji Tourism (www.fiji.travel) before making plans.

CALENDAR OF SPECIAL EVENTS

January
New Year's, nationwide – The turn of the year is a big deal in Fiji, where celebrations go on for a week, and sometimes even longer.

February/March
Holi, nationwide – Although not a public holiday, the Hindu 'Festival of Colours' is enthusiastically, vividly and messily celebrated.

March/April
Easter, nationwide – Good Friday, Easter

An honour guard ahead of Fiji's 45th anniversary of independence in 2015

Sunday and Easter Monday are all public holidays. Leading up to Easter is the seven-day Fijian Crosswalk, where a cross is carried, accompanied by reverent crowds, from Suva to Nadi.

July/August
Bula Festival, Nadi – A week-long festival with daily entertainment, culminating in a procession of floats, brass bands, marching contingents and beauty queens through the streets of Nadi. Festival grounds have an amusement park with carnival rides.

South Indian fire-walking festival, Mariamma Temple, Suva – Timed to coincide with the full moon, this Hindu tradition sees men walking barefoot over blazing embers, after following a strict diet and abstaining from sex for 10 days, and having had their tongue and cheeks pierced by a priest with skewers.

August
Hibiscus Festival, Suva – In a nice reversal of fate, this began as something for the tourists and has morphed into a week of fun for locals. The festival features a program of nightly entertainment and culminates in a procession of floats through the streets of Suva and a grand finale at Albert Park on Saturday night when the new hibiscus queen, acknowledged as Fiji's loveliest, is chosen.

Festival of the Friendly North, Labasa, Vanua Levu – A cheery, 40-year old festival in the same vein as the Sugar and Bula festivals, with a friendly king and queen being crowned, all aimed at increasing awareness of the region as a welcoming place to visit.

September
Sugar City Festival, Lautoka – A week of festivities in the town that was built from refined sweetness, where a sugar king and queen are eventually crowned.

Coral Coast Festival, Sigatoka – A coming together of the coral coast's communities and tourists, with activities and events to celebrate the coast's beauty and history.

10 October
Fiji Day, nationwide – A joint celebration on the anniversary of Fiji's cession to the United Kingdom in 1874, and the subsequent declaration of independence in 1970. Fiji Week, seven days of religious and cultural ceremonies celebrating the country's diversity, happens just before Fiji Day, which is a public holiday. The 50th Anniversary of Fiji Week lands in 2020.

October/November
Diwali, nationwide – A traditional Hindu festival of lights, held in honour of Lakshmi, the goddess of wealth and prosperity. Thousands of clay lamps are lit by Hindu devotees around homes throughout the country as people dress up in their best clothes to visit each other and exchange gifts of sweets. Some of the wealthy merchants in town also festoon their homes with displays of flashing electric lights.

HISTORY: KEY DATES

Prior to the arrival of Europeans, indigenous Fijians had no written language, and historical events were passed down orally, often assuming legendary status with the passage of time and repeated retelling.

BEFORE THE EUROPEANS

c.1500 BC	The islands that now comprise Fiji are settled. Debate still rages between anthropologists over whether these first people were of Melanesian or Polynesian extraction. Either way, the earliest known inhabitants are now referred to as the 'Lapita people' after a style of pottery they produced, which was found in the area from 800 BC.
c.500 BC	The local population, now a mix of Polynesian and Melanesian, begin to rely more on agriculture, which increases land pressure and intertribal fighting. The practice of cannibalism is traced to this time.
1000 AD	The islands of Fiji are first invaded by their Pacific neighbours, the Tongans. Warfare between the islands carries on sporadically for centuries.

EUROPEAN ARRIVALS

1643	En route back from New Zealand, where he'd just made first contact with the Maoris, Dutch explorer Abel Tasman spots the northern islands of Fiji, becoming the first European to do so. He doesn't make landfall.
1774	Captain James Cook sails through the region, recording the presence of the islands and forever branding them with the name Fiji – a phonetic spelling of the mispronounced word the Tongans use for the islands.
1789	Having suffered a mutiny and been cast adrift from his ship, *The Bounty*, Captain Bligh passes through the Yasawa Islands in a small boat with 17 loyal crewmembers. After an earlier incident on the tiny island of Tofua, where a man was killed, he declines to land – a decision vindicated when canoes pursue his boat.

Levuka in 1885

	Despite all this, Bligh manages to make a detailed map of the islands' coast.
1792	Bligh returns in the vessel HMS *Providence*.
1797	The London Missionary Society's ship *Duff* enters Fiji from the north and strikes Heemskirk Reef.
1800	American schooner Argo is wrecked in Lau. The surviving crew bring a devastating epidemic, killing thousands of Fijians.
1822	A rudimentary European settlement is established by whalers at Levuka.
1830	Christian missionaries begin to arrive at Lakeba from Tahiti, Hatai, Arue and Tahaara, encouraged and assisted by the London Missionary Society.
1845	The chief of Viwa, Ratu Ravisa (Varani), converts to Christianity under the influence of Reverend John Hunt, a major success for the missionaries.
1847	Tongan Prince Enele Ma'afu arrives in Fiji and builds a settlement in Lakeba.
1849	A trading store set up by American settler and de facto US Consul John Brown Williams is accidentally destroyed by stray cannon fire, and then looted of its contents by Fijians.
1851	The US navy begin demanding compensation from Fijians for Williams' losses.

BIRTH OF A NATION

1853	Ratu Seru Epenisa Cakobau, a local warlord, declares himself Vunivalu (Paramount Chief) of Bau, and Tui Viti (King of Fiji). His claim is not accepted by other chiefs, and a series of conflicts begin.
1854	Cakobau converts to Christianity and renounces cannibalism.
1855	With the help of the Tongans, Cakobau defeats his enemies from Rewa and Bau in the Battle of Kaba, strengthening his leadership over Fiji, but underlining his dependency on Tonga.
1855	As the US Navy continue to aggressively pursue compensation for the destruction of Williams' store, Cakobau attempts to cede Fiji to the British in return for money to pay off the Americans. The UK passes up the offer, realising that Cakobau lacks the full authority to offer them the islands.

Prince Charles hands over independence to Fiji

1865	The chiefs come together to form the Confederacy of Independent Kingdoms of Viti, and Cakobau becomes Chairman of the General Assembly.
1867	The confederacy splits into the Kingdom of Bau and the Confederation of Lau. Cakobau assumes kingship of Bau. Meanwhile, with the debt for Williams' store still unpaid, the US navy threaten to shell Levuka with a warship.
1868	The Australian Polynesia Company, an Australian-based company, pays the debts to the US, in return for land near Suva.
1871	The Kingdom of Fiji is established, with Cakobau on the throne in the capital of Levuka, but much power concentrated in the hands of the foreigners who bailed him out of trouble with the Americans.
1874	After the new kingdom gets into debt, the British government bankrolls Cakobau, and he cedes the title of Tui Viti (Paramount Chief of Fiji) to Queen Victoria (a title now held by Queen Elizabeth II, as far as the current chiefs of Fiji are concerned). Fiji becomes part of the British Empire.
1875	A measles epidemic kills a third of the Fijian population.
1879	The first 463 indentured labourers from India arrive and begin work on the plantations. In the next 37 years, 61,000 more follow.
1882	The British move Fiji's capital city from Levuka to Suva.
1916	The controversial practise of importing indentured labourers from India to Fiji to work on plantations comes to an end.
1939	Nadi Airport built as an air base by the Allied powers as World War II erupts.
1970	10 October, Fiji attains independence, ending 96 years of British rule.

THE LATE 20TH CENTURY

1987	13 April, The general election is won by the Labour-National Federation Party coalition, installing Timoci Bavadra as Prime Minister.
1987	14 May, Lieutenant Colonel Sitiveni Rabuka carries out a coup d'état, toppling Bavadra from power.
1987	7 October, Rabuka proclaims Fiji a republic, severing the 113-year link to the British Monarchy, removing the queen as head of state

Commodore Frank Bainimarama in 2006

and installing Ratu Sir Penaia Ganilau as Fiji's first President. As a result of the coup, Fiji is expelled from the Commonwealth of Nations and isn't readmitted for 10 years.

1992 Following new elections, Rabuka becomes Prime Minister.

1999 The Fiji Labour Party (FLP) triumph in a general election, and Mahendra Chaudhry becomes Fiji's first Prime Minister of Indian descent.

THE MODERN ERA

2000 19 May, A civilian coup d'état, instigated by George Speight, topples the Chaudhry government; 36 members of parliament are kidnapped and some are held until 13 July. President Mara attempts to support Chaudhry, but on 29 May, Commodore Bainimarama, Commander of Fiji's Military, takes over the presidency. Violent scenes take place in Suva, Levuka, Naitasiri, Tailevu, Ra, Nadi, Yasawa, Serua, Namosi and Vanua Levu.

2001 August, Democracy is restored. Speight is subsequently sentenced to death after pleading guilty to a charge of treason, but his sentence is commuted to life imprisonment.

2004 Professional golfer Vijay Singh, an Indo-Fijian who was born in Lautoka and grew up in Nadi, becomes the World's number one golfer – a position he holds for 32 weeks.

2006 5 December, Commodore Bainimarama instigates a coup, bringing down the government of Laisenia Qarase and declaring himself Acting President of Fiji.

2009 Fiji is expelled from the Commonwealth after refusing to bow to international demands to hold democratic elections.

2014 September, Bainimarama's FijiFirst Party wins the first general elections held since 2006, during a process declared as properly democratic by international observers. Fiji's suspension from the Commonwealth is lifted.

2016 In February, Tropical Cyclone Winston – officially the strongest ever recorded in the southern hemisphere – batters the country, leaving 42 dead and tens of thousands forced from their homes.

2018 November, Fijians vote in the general election, with Bainimarama's FijiFirst Party emerging victorious. There is a rise in the number of female politicians elected.

BEST ROUTES

Arriving by catamaran

MAMANUCA ISLANDS

There's no better way to get a feel for Fiji than by hitching a lift on a short cruise or light plane flight from Nadi to the nearby Mamanuca Islands, to rinse away your jetlag on the beaches of this scattering of idyllic South Pacific jewels.

DISTANCE: 25 miles (40km) by ferry
TIME: 3 days (or more)
START/END: Denarau
POINTS TO NOTE: There are various ways of getting out to the islands, from cheap and cheerful multi-stop ferries, to bespoke-itinerary cruises aboard luxury yachts, and scenic flights in light aircraft (to Mana). Most boats depart from Denarau Island, which is connected to the main island and is easily reached by bus or taxi from Nadi. Organised trips almost always include hotel pick-up from the city. Some boats leave from Lautoka.

Fiji is not a place to be in a rush, but the quickest and easiest way to get a taste of the sun-splattered desert-island destination you're almost certainly expecting to encounter, is to leave Nadi quick-smart and head towards the **Mamanuca Islands**, just off the mainland of Viti Levu.

There are 20 islands in this group (although some disappear at high tide), where around 18 resorts and myriad tour companies cater for a range of tastes and budgets. But regardless of whether you're travelling on a shoestring or a yacht, everything revolves around three common denominators: sun, sea and sand – all of which are readily available here.

The Mamanucas have starred in films (Monuriki Island was Tom Hanks' lonely paradise in *Cast Away*) and on TV *(Survivor – Fiji)*, and they are exactly what you imagine when you hear the words 'tropical' and 'island' used in the same sentence. In between these South Pacific punctuation points, brilliant scuba diving can be enjoyed at such famous sites as Gotham City (named after the batfish that frequent it) and Big W, and there's even a world-class surf break (Fiji's best).

Buses pick up guests from hotels all around Nadi and from the various resorts on the Coral Coast, and deliver them to the port on Denarau Island, which is connected to the mainland, ready for transfer onto the bustling boats. Once loaded, various vessels skim across the waters of the South Pacific – generally quite calm within the protective embrace of Malolo Barrier Reef – out to the islands.

Also known as Monuriki   *Sunset at Castaway Island*

INDEPENDENT ISLAND-HOPPING

While there are plenty of predetermined group itineraries, a great way to discover these islands is to build your own single- or multi-day adventure by travelling out to the islands with **Awesome Adventures Fiji** (tel: 675 0499; www.awesomefiji. com) on the *Yasawa Flyer*, which calls twice daily at several islands in the group, whilst travelling to and from the further flung Yasawa Islands (see page 64). Single- and multi-trip ticket options make it possible to concentrate on one island, or the Bula Pass allows you to freestyle your way around the islands on the route,

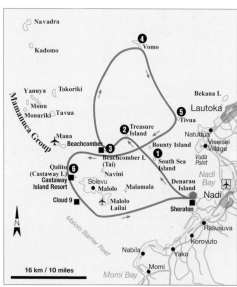

with tickets spanning from five to 15 days available.

After leaving Denarau Marina at 8.30am each morning, the *Yasawa Flyer*'s Mamanuca stops include sandy **South Sea Island ❶**, a backpacker-friendly option with *bure*-based accommodation, a restaurant and bar, and plenty of aquatic adventures to keep everyone happy; **Treasure Island ❷** (Elevuka; www.treas-ureisland-fiji.com), a verdant green isle, ringed with white sands, which has a family friendly, locally-owned resort offering various activities; **Beachcomber ❸** (Tai; www.beachcomberfiji.com), a resort-dominated sand-encircled islet that attracts a young party-happy crowd and offers a range of watersports; and **Vomo ❹** (https://vomofiji.com) a private luxury resort island with kayaking, stand-up paddle boarding, windsurfing and snorkelling all offered. Scuba diving lessons are also available. There is also a small mountain with hiking paths and a nine-hole golf course. Day trips are not available here.

The distinctive yellow catamaran then heads off into the heart of the Yasawa group, before turning around at the Blue Lagoon and stopping off at all the same

Seaplane taking off from Cloud 9

islands again, arriving back to Denarau at 5.45pm. At each stop, small boats come racing out from the islands to pick up those who are alighting from the ferry, and drop off those who are boarding. It's worth doing it for the trip alone. Reservations are best made in advance in high season.

Flight of fancy

Taking a boat trip out to the islands across the big blue blanket of the South Pacific Ocean is a sensational experience, but it is extremely hard to beat a nostalgic flight in a seaplane. Skimming at low altitude over the translucent sea and sand encircled islets of the Mamanuca Group and enjoying a bird of paradise's eye peak at the coral curves of Malolo Barrier Reef is something you'll never forget, and if you're only ever going to take a seaplane flight once, this is the place. You can even go one way in a seaplane and return in a helicopter, landing on an island of your choice for a luxury lunch, or calling in for a cocktail and a pizza on Cloud 9 (see page 91). And it isn't quite as indulgent as you might think, with scenic and combination flights from Nadi starting from around F$520.

Pacific Island Air (tel: 672 5644; www.pacificislandair.com) flies to many Mamanuca Group islands, and pretty much all the Yasawas too. You can even fly with your surfboard.

DAY TRIPPING

Many visitors prefer to spend their entire holiday in one resort, but day cruises are a great option for travellers who want to see a bit more of Fiji. Day trips leave each morning (usually 9–10am) and return late in the afternoon (about 5–6pm), and your options are manifold.

With **Captain Cook Cruises** (tel: 670 1823; www.captaincookcruisesfiji.com) you can sail to sand-fringed, reef-ringed **Tivua Island** ❺, a tiny teardrop of a coral cay, aboard a tall ship (the Ra *Marama*) or a sailing catamaran (*Fiji One*). **South Sea Cruises** (tel: 675 0500; www.ssc.com.fj) offer half-day and full-day trips to **South Sea Island**, and full-day trips to the Fijian family–owned and lagoon-blessed **Malolo**, and exclusive **Castaway Island** ❻ (real name Qalito, just off Malolo), a delightful cliché of a tropical island, where only 10 day-trippers are allowed at a time.

One interesting option, which is competitively priced (considering the sybaritic feel of the experience), is a trip on the **Whale's Tale** (www.whalestale.com.fj), a beautiful schooner-rigged motor yacht, which sails past Malamala, Vunavadra, Bounty and Treasure Islands within the Mamanuca group, en route to uninhabited Schooner Island, with a champagne breakfast to enjoy on the way.

Prices vary, but most cruises cost around F$200–250 per adult per day, which should include lunch, use of snorkelling equipment and some water activities (scuba diving always costs extra).

Garden of the Sleeping Giant

GARDEN OF THE SLEEPING GIANT AND VISEISEI VILLAGE

Escape Nadi to explore the Garden of the Sleeping Giant, with its abundant orchids;
Viseisei Village, where you can score a glimpse of traditional life in the country's oldest
settlement; and the sugar-producing city of Lautoka, Fiji's second-largest city.

DISTANCE: 20 miles (30km) each way
TIME: A full day
START: Nadi
END: Lautoka
POINTS TO NOTE: This route requires the use of a car. If you don't want to drive yourself, the Garden of the Sleeping Giant is close enough to Nadi to visit by taxi. The Garden of the Sleeping Giant is found on the Wailoko Road – 4 miles (6.5km) north of the airport – an easy 25-minute car ride from Nadi. The garden is open all year round, and tours are included in the entry fee.

There's nothing wrong with Nadi, per se, but it's unlikely to be the slice of tropical paradise you had in mind when you booked your Fijian foray. It's a functional metropolis for locals, but for visitors it's a transport hub – a place to land and then leave. Just beyond the sprawling suburbs of the city, however, are several places well worth exploring; this route links three of the best.

GARDEN OF THE SLEEPING GIANT

Leaving Nadi, head north along Queens Road towards Lautoka. Drive past the airport (on your left) and after 3 miles (5km) you will arrive at the Wailoko Road turn-off. Look for a sign on a lamppost on the right-hand side, and then turn right into Wailoko Road. Drive another mile (1.6km) to the entrance of the garden on your left.

A visit to the **Garden of the Sleeping Giant** ❶ (Wailoko Road; tel: 672 3418; www.gsgfiji.com; Mon–Sat 9am–5pm, Sun until noon) is an unforgettable experience, regardless of whether you consider yourself a flower fan or not. Gawping at over 150,000 Asian orchids and Cattleya hybrids, spread across 2,000 species (at least 30 of which are native to Fiji), flora adorers will find themselves in horticultural heaven, but everyone will appreciate this blissfully serene and beautiful spot on some level.

Occupying 20 hectares (50 acres) of gently sloping land at the base of the Sabeto Range, the garden takes its name from the apparent silhouette of a giant who appears to be asleep on top of the

Two men in traditional Fijian dress outside a typical village house in Viseisei

mountains. It started in 1977, with a personal collection of orchids grown by the American actor Raymond Burr (from the television series *Ironside*), but the garden has been completely replanted since then, after being destroyed by cyclones.

An attractive reception centre in the style of a Fijian *bure* with a verandah facing the valley has comfortable cane furniture for visitors. Here, you can sit and admire the view, sip on a cool drink of fruit juice which comes with the admission fee, and then either stroll through the gardens yourself or enjoy an informative guided tour.

The entire property is a kaleidoscope of colour, with a profusion of orchids everywhere you go. A long walk through one shade house leads to a pond of water lilies, a bridge and a rest area, and then continues through jungle interplanted with flowering trees and shrubs. There are numerous seats where you can relax and absorb your sensational surrounds.

A little further east along the road from the garden is **Sabeto Hotspring** ❷ (daily 7am–6pm), with a series of naturally heated pools and mud baths available overlooked by the peaks of Koroyanitu National Heritage Park.

VISEISEI VILLAGE

Allow 20 minutes for your drive from Sabeto Hotspring to **Viseisei Village** ❸ (daily 7am–6pm). According to legends, the ancestors of today's Fijians first arrived at Vuda Point nearby, and the village has played a large role in the formation and politics of the modern nation. Viseisei was once home to Fijian Prime Minister Dr Timoci Bavadra (who was deposed in a military coup in 1987), and the late Chief of Viseisei, Ratu Josefa Iloilo, who was president of Fiji from 2000 to 2009.

Take a left turn immediately after the bridge at the signpost. You'll know you have arrived because of the road humps on the Queens Road highway.

Viseisei Village has

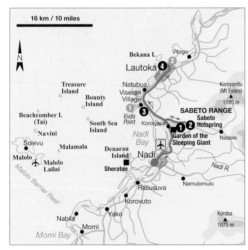

Lautoka harbour and sugar mill

been open to the public for more than 30 years, and this is a great opportunity to meet local people on their own turf and see something of their way of life. Villagers will happily show you around, and it is appropriate to give a small gratuity (F$5) to your guide before leaving. The large **Jone Wesele (John Wesley) Church**, with a memorial commemorating the centenary of the arrival of missionaries in Fiji in 1835, is a point of interest.

Turn off to the Vuda Marina at the top of the hill for a light lunch at **The Boatshed Restaurant and Sunset Bar**, see ❶.

LAUTOKA

Continue north along Queens Road, through Lauwaki, to the harbour city of **Lautoka** ❹, from where the southern Yasawa Islands are visible on the near horizon.

Now Fiji's second largest city, with a population of 52,000, Lautoka owes its existence primarily to a deepwater port and a huge **sugar mill**, once the biggest in the Southern Hemisphere, which you can walk to along Marine Drive (there's no official tour, but it's interesting to watch the action as sugar, molasses and woodchips are loaded onto boats). Some of the finest sugar in the world is produced here, and the city throws a weeklong Sugar Festival each September, where a Sugar Queen and Sugar King are crowned.

While there isn't an abundance of things to see in Lautoka – beyond some nice parks and the sugarcane railway

that runs through the centre of the town between a line of tall royal palm trees – the city has some of the best value accommodation to be found in Fiji, and there's also a few decent places to eat, too. Try **The Chilli Tree Café**, see ❷, before heading back to Nadi.

Food and drink

❶ THE BOATSHED RESTAURANT & SUNSET BAR

Vuda Marina; tel: 666 8214; www.vudamarina.com.fj; daily 10am–10pm; $$
The location is sensational – unsurprisingly the Sunset Bar is a great spot for a sundowner – and the Boatshed menu is comprehensive and inviting, making the most of delicious local ingredients. Think Kokoda Salad (poached local fish in lime juice and coconut milk) and homemade seafood chowder served in a herb bread roll. Pizzas are also available – including one with a lobster topping. There's also a play area for the kids.

❷ THE CHILLI TREE CAFÉ

Tukani Street, Lautoka; tel: 665 1824; Mon–Sat 8am–5pm; $
Breakfasts here are big and generous, whether you go for the bacon and eggs option or roll with the pancakes. The coffee (both iced and hot variety) is good. You'll also find substantial sandwiches (something of a rarity in Fiji) and juicy burgers, making this a great lunchtime stop. Free Wi-Fi is a bonus too.

NATADOLA BEACH PICNIC AND CORAL COAST RAILWAY

Go south from Nadi to see the historic Momi Bay Guns, enjoy a picnic at popular Natadola Beach, ride the cute Coral Coast Railway, and visit Sigatoka's spectacular sand dunes.

DISTANCE: 55 miles (88km) each way
TIME: A full day
START: Nadi
END: Sigatoka
POINTS TO NOTE: This route requires the use of a car – see page 98 for more information about how to hire vehicles and things you should know about driving in Fiji. Natadola is a beautiful surf-stroked beach, but be aware that there are undercurrents – people who are not strong swimmers, and those with children, should take care. Keep an eye on your valuables on the beach, too.

Pack a hearty picnic lunch and drive out of town, heading south along Queens Road towards Suva, in search of Viti Levu's best beach and a slice of history.

MOMI GUNS

The first point of interest is found 9 miles (15km) along the road at the Momi Bay turn-off, where a sign proclaims a place of historic interest: the site of the **Momi Bay Guns ❶** (daily 9am–5pm). Initially installed by the 30th Battalion of the New Zealand Expeditionary Forces, and later manned by the American army, these guns were set up here in 1941 to defend the southern approach to Nandi Bay from Japanese attack during World War II. They have been restored by the National Trust of Fiji, and signposts point the way. For obvious reasons, the guns are positioned with a commanding view over Momi Bay and the main channel in the barrier reef, and visitors can enjoy a beautiful vista of the nearby Mamanuca Islands.

NATADOLA BEACH

Return to the main road and continue south towards Suva. It takes about 25 minutes to reach the Natadola Beach turn-off at Maro Road, some 25 miles (40km) from Nadi. Maro Road is clearly signposted and the turn-off is easy to find as there is a mosque on the left and a Hindu temple just above the turn-off on the right. This is still the heart of the sugar cane growing area and the road twists and winds its way to the sea between sugar

Natadola Beach

cane farms and mosques. You cross the river twice, and this will confirm that you are on the right road.

Allow 15 minutes for a comfortable drive from the turn-off before arriving at **Natadola Beach ❷**, where a magnificent arc of bright white sand curves for more than a mile, starting from Navo Island in the south. The prevailing tradewind comes off the land so that the extensive bay is usually calm and ideal for wind-surfing. Coral reefs encompass the bay to nearly a mile offshore, where a wide passage allows safe entry into the bay. Yachtsmen tend to avoid this anchorage because the wide entrance allows a swell from the south to roll into the bay causing boats to rock uncomfortably. But the same swell sometimes produces conditions ideal for body surfing.

The beach is popular with locals, who congregate here on weekends picnicking or enjoying barbecues. Coral reefs on each side of the bay offer good snorkelling but the main feature is simply the exquisite expanse of white sand. Locals often offer horse-riding experiences along the beach.

CORAL COAST RAILWAY

For a ride of a different kind and a pre-ar-

Tropical train ride

The Coral Coast Railway is part of a network that was originally established by the Colonial Sugar Refining Company when it developed Fiji's sugar industry. Historically the trains hauled raw sugarcane along narrow-gauge tracks to Lautoka for processing, and when the Fiji government purchased the company in 1970, the railway system was maintained. Today, sugar cane is still taken to Lautoka on this line, but ever since an enterprising New Zealander decided to build period coaches and a terminal station, the little trains also transport tourists to and from Natadola Beach.

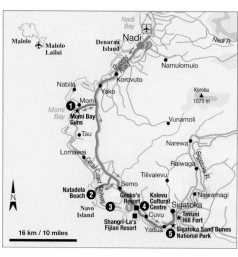

Coral Coast Railway

ranged picnic, continue on the main highway for another 15 minutes to the terminal of the cute narrow-gauge **Coral Coast Railway** ❸ (daily; tel: 652 0434) accessed via the turn-off for the Shangri-La's Fijian Resort.

From here, the family-friendly Coral Coast train departs at l0am and reaches Natadola Beach just before noon. It chugs along the track beside the lagoon, through countryside only accessible by the train. A barbecue lunch is served and there is enough time for swimming, snorkelling and horse riding before the departure at 2.30pm for the 1-hour ride back.

CUVU CULTURE CLUB

If you haven't previously had a chance to visit a real village, the **Kalevu Cultural Centre** ❹ (Queens Road, near Cuvu; tel: 652 0200; one-hour and half-day tours) is worth a look. This is a recreated Fijian village, where you can explore traditional style *bures*, learn about local history, culture, traditions and crafts, such pottery making, and experience a kava drinking ceremony and tap cloth demonstrations.

If you haven't already demolished a barbecue lunch on the train, or you're looking for an evening meal with entertainment, try **Gecko's Restaurant**, see ❶, nearby.

SIGATOKA SAND DUNES

Continue another 6 miles (10km) to **Sigatoka Sand Dunes National Park** ❺ (daily 8am–5pm), one of Fiji's most arresting sights and the country's first national park. A visitor centre just off the main road on the right has displays and a walkway with vistas. For a proper eyeful of the sensational sandscape, get closer and ascend the dunes – which stretch for 3 miles (5km) and soar up to 200ft (30 metres) at their western extremity, offering panoramic views of the ocean and the Sigatoka River estuary. Some of Fiji's most important archaeological discoveries have been made in these sands. The winds constantly expose pottery shards and, sometimes, even human remains – indeed the oldest human bones found in the Polynesian Pacific came from this site.

The exposed beach is a haunt for surfers and windsurfers, but only strong swimmers and experienced surfers should venture into the sea here.

Food and drink

❶ GECKO'S RESTAURANT

Queens Road; tel: 652 0200; www. geckosresort.com; 8am–late; $$
The menu here boasts a broad range of international dishes, but really, why go past the seafood when it's this fresh and fantastic? Prices are reasonable, and you can grab a drink by the pool before lunching on lobster. On weekend evenings you'll score entertainment from fire dancers and others whilst you munch.

Sigatoka Sand Dunes National Park

NADI TO SUVA

Travel from Fiji's travel hub to the country's charming capital city of Suva, via the epic Queen's Road, driving past scenic sugarcane fields, forests of lush Caribbean pine trees, sensational sand dunes, isolated bays, historic hillforts, friendly villages and fancy resorts.

DISTANCE: 122 miles (197km) each way

TIME: A full day

START: Nadi

END: Suva

POINTS TO NOTE: This route requires the use of a car; see page 98 for information about car hire and Fijian road rules. Because of the distance you will be covering and the spectacular scenery along the way, a self-drive day trip to Suva should begin early in the morning; an 8am start is ideal. The road is well maintained and sealed all the way. This journey will require at least 3 hours of driving, plus stops for photography on the way. Allow extra time to visit Sigatoka Sand Dunes National Park (see route 3), Tavuni Hill Fort and Kula Eco Park. This should have you arriving in Suva for an early dinner, after which you can drive back to Nadi or spend the night in Suva.

This drive covers the Garden Route of Viti Levu. It follows Queens Road through the sand-dune and surf beach-flanked town of Sigatoka to the Coral Coast, which you then trace all the way to Pacific Harbour, threading a line between lush verdant hills to your left, and the iridescent South Pacific on your right. The water is calmed by the presence of an off-shore reef, which forms lagoons along the way.

SIGATOKA AND SURROUNDS

Pick up Queens Road in Nadi and follow it out of town heading south, through Korovuto, Yako and Semo to Sigatoka. If you haven't followed route 3 (see page 44), allow some time to explore the highly impressive **Sigatoka Sand Dunes National Park** ❶ (daily 8am–5pm), a series of epically proportioned waves of sand west of Sigatoka town, which stand 20 metres high and stretch for miles. Burial sites and ancient artefacts have been uncovered here, but it's also a great big playground where you can try sand surfing.

Follow the road as it skirts the estuary and takes you into the town of

Along the Queen's Road

Sigatoka ②, a pleasant little place on the banks of Fiji's second largest river, which is home to a large farming community and forms a gateway to the tourist resorts along the Coral Coast.

There's not too much to see in the town itself, but **Tavuni Hill Fort ③** (Mon–Sat 8am–5pm), an impressive defensive structure built by exiled Tongan chief Maile Latamai in the 18th century, is worth a visit. It's on the eastern side of the Sigatoka River, above Naroro village. To get there, cross the bridge and take the first left turn, which will bring you back to the river and the old bridge. Turn right at the old bridge and follow the river upstream; it's about 2 miles (4km) from the turn-off. After exploring, return to the first bridge and continue east along the coast.

For an alternative, adventurous inland route back to Nadi, see page 54.

CORAL COAST

The stretch of road between Korotogo and Naboutini is particularly attractive. It winds around bays and climbs low ridges for views of villages and lagoons glimpsed through avenues of coconut palms and rainforest, and then moves away from the coast, climbs a series of low hills and emerges on the coast to briefly join the sea again before reaching the wide expanse of open, flat land at Pacific Harbour. The islands of Yanuca and Beqa are visible offshore.

About 4 miles (7km) past the Sigatoka River bridge is the village of Korotogo, where the highway joins

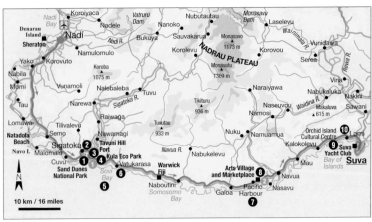

In Kula Eco Park

the Coral Coast. From here, the road runs for 21 miles (35km) right beside the lagoon and through a series of villages and resorts. Korotogo marks the southern boundary of the sugar cane-growing area, and the landscape begins to change as you head southeast, with rainforest stretching over hills and mountains as far as the eye can see, well watered by moisture dropped from clouds pushed along by the prevailing tradewinds.

Numerous hotels rub shoulders in Korotogo, from big resorts to smaller, more intimate hotels, which cater for every type of budget and taste. Children and wildlife lovers will enjoy the excellent **Kula Eco Park** ❹ (tel: 650 0505; www.fijiwild.com; daily 10am–4.30pm, last entry 4pm), where you can meet a marvellous menagerie of native bird, reptile and marine life while exploring 12 acres of land, wandering along boardwalks at your own pace, or by taking a tour. For lunch, hit Sunset Strip and try **Beach Bar n' Grill**, see ❶.

The road skirts around Bulu Bay and then goes around the bigger and more open **Sovi Bay** ❺, where there's a popular beach. This is a good place for a break and a swim – but do be careful of the currents. There are parking places by the side of the road and plenty of picnicking spots.

Further east, the village of **Vatukarasa** ❻ is laid out in traditional Fijian style, with a handsome chief's *bure* next to the road as you first enter, a wide village green with houses and *bures* on each side, and a church at the other end. Vatukarasa Bay is wide and at times allows a big swell to roll in and crash onto the beach.

Continuing on you will pass the resorts of Tambua Sands, the Hideaway and Naviti, each tucked away among flowers and coconut trees next to its own beach, before reaching Korolevu, the site of Fiji's first beach resort. At the other end of the bay is the Warwick Fiji, a luxury 28-acre resort.

PACIFIC HARBOUR

When it was created, **Pacific Harbour** ❼ was one of Fiji's most ambitious projects. Several hundred acres of lowland were cleared and drained, lakes were created and an 18-hole championship golf course designed by Robert Trent Jones Jr was built. Swish accommodation options such as the Pearl South Pacific were constructed beside the beach, and a culture and shopping centre was built around one of the lakes.

With staged performances in a touristy setting, it's not everyone's cup of kava, but caters very well for families and bus tours, and if you're into golf and/or scuba diving (Beqa Lagoon offers world-class diving), you'll find plenty to do. Check out the **Arts Village and Marketplace** ❽ (tel: 345

Weaving palm leaves at the Arts Village and Marketplace

0065; www.artsvillage.com.fj; Mon–Sat 9am–4pm, check show times online) for souvenirs, packaged culture, *lovo* lunches, and fire-walking and *meke* shows. If you feel yourself flagging, grab a cracking coffee and some banana bread from **Skinny Bean Cafe**, see ❷.

Food and drink

❶ BEACH BAR N' GRILL

Sunset Strip, Korotongo; tel: 902 5979; daily 3–9.30pm; $

Good prices, fantastically fresh ingredients, super-friendly service and a beautiful location add up to make this chilled-out little eatery an ace place to fill your face. Dive into the garlic chilli prawns or the fresh-caught lobster served in a coconut, chased down by a cocktail.

❷ SKINNY BEAN CAFE

Shop 5B Arts Village, Pacific Harbour; tel: 385 9869; http://skinnybeancafe. restaurantsnapshot.com; Mon–Sat 7am–7pm, Sun until 4pm; $

There are several resort-style restaurants and bars in Pacific Harbour, but if you're just looking for a restorative shot of caffeine and a snack, hop into this harbour-front cafe, which serves sublime coffee and brilliant banana bread. Some more substantial options are also available.

SUVA AND SUBURBS

From Pacific Harbour, the road runs through a wide plain, the monotony broken by immense banyan trees, grazing cattle, maize and sorghum plantations, and rice paddies flourishing over the wide expanse of fertile land. The township of Navua is on the eastern bank of the river where land is held in small-holdings by Indian farmers who specialise in rice cultivation.

On the outskirts of Suva, you'll pass the **Orchid Island Cultural Centre** ❾ (Mon–Sat 6am–8pm), which reopened in 2016. The site is dedicated to demonstrating traditional arts and crafts. There is also a small museum about the country's more gruesome old customs and rituals and information about the regional flora and fauna.

About 2 miles (4km) before you reach the capital, you'll skirt the Bay of Islands and the attractive suburb of **Lami** ❿. A Novotel Hotel sits on the water's edge here, where yachts and pleasure craft bob in the bay in the lee of three islands, and there is a convention centre beside the lagoon. En route to the heart of the city, you then pass through the Walu Bay industrial area and the Royal Suva Yacht Club.

You can either opt to spend the night at Suva (see page 77 for accommodation and page 84 for eating options) and tour the colourful town the following morning, or if you arrive early, tour Suva and then drive back to Nadi.

Renwick Road in Suva

SUVA

Take in the city sights during this half-day tour of Fiji's capital city of Suva, and revel in a melting pot of diverse cultures, each with their own colourful cuisines and customs.

DISTANCE: 3.5 miles (5.5km)
TIME: A half day
START/END: Thurston Gardens
POINTS TO NOTE: The distance and time given here does not include the additional wander around the peninsula to the university campus. There are markets in several locations in Suva, some better than others – as always, the old adage caveat emptor applies: when buying souvenirs it's well worth investing the time to find out where and how things were made, rather than just going for the cheapest option. Be prepared to bargain, but pay a fair price for genuine handcrafted artefacts.

Suva isn't just the capital of Fiji, it's also the largest city in the South Pacific – but don't go expecting to find a gritty metropolis. This is a typical tropical town, buzzing with a friendly and welcoming vibe, but on a much bigger scale (and with a slightly more business-like spring in its step). Perched on a peninsula poking into the Pacific, it has verdant municipal gardens and a fabulous foreshore to explore, as well as a wonderfully intricate mosaic of cultures and influences to taste and touch. All of Fiji's fantastic diversity is represented on these streets, which are lined with curry restaurants, sarong shops and hipster student hangouts.

GARDEN ROUTE

This route begins in the botanical bosom of **Thurston Gardens** ❶ (daily), where you will find a large and interesting collection of flora from around the South Pacific. Within the grounds of the gardens, you'll also discover the **Fiji Museum** ❷ (tel: 331 5944; www.fijimuseum.org.fj; Mon–Thu and Sat 9am–4.30pm, Fri until 4pm). Established in 1904, the museum is a gem. It holds the most comprehensive collection of Fijian artefacts in existence, as well as a collection of curiosities from other Pacific islands. A double-hulled canoe that was built in 1900 – and used in the making of the movie *His Majesty O'Keefe*, starring Burt Lancaster – commands your attention in the main hall.

Fiji Museum

Wander through the gardens or walk west along Cakobau Road until you hit Victoria Parade/Queen Elizabeth Drive. Turn left on Queen Elizabeth Drive, to check out the gates of Government House, the state residence of the President of Fiji. A guard dressed in a red tunic and white *sulu* (sarong) at the gate is a favourite subject for a photograph here.

SEAFRONT STROLL

If you continue along the seafront far enough, you will eventually round the peninsula and reach the Suva campus of the **University of the South Pacific**, built on a former seaplane base. This base played a critical role in the Pacific theatre of action during WWII, helping to repel the threat of a Japanese invasion by mounting long-range reconnaissance missions, and performing mercy flights, which saved many lives. The **ANZ Stadium,** where the Fijian national rugby team plays, is also nearby.

Retrace your steps back up Queen Elizabeth Drive until it segues into the main drag of Victoria Parade. Go past Thurston Gardens and Albert Park on your right, and a lawn bowling club on your left. If you're hungry, turn right on Macarthur Street and call into **Bad Dog Café**, see ❶, by Suva's legendary nightspot, O'Reilly's, for a pizza.

THE CBD

Retrace your steps to Victoria Parade, turn right and continue north. At the end of

the block, cross Townhall Road and keep going straight, with Ratu Sukuna Park on your left. Victoria Parade becomes Scott Street and meets Renwick Road at a Y junction, with an old ivi (native chestnut) tree in the triangle. Much of old Suva still survives in Renwick Road.

At the next junction, turn right into Thomson Street, where the old vies with the new, follow the road across Nabukalou Creek and turn right again into Cumming Street. On this corner, one of the oldest and least changed parts of Suva,

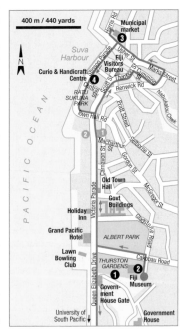

Kava seller at the market

Shops in Cumming Street

you'll often encounter Fijian women selling handicrafts under a flamboyant tree, and duty-free dealers hawking their wares.

GOING TO MARKET

Stroll up Cumming Street, turn left into Renwick Road and then turn left again into Marks Street, which will take you past the Thomson Street junction. Continue down along Usher Street to the **Municipal Market** ❸ (Mon–Thu 7am–5pm, Fri and Sat from 6am). Along with the adjoining bus-stand, this market covers an entire city block and offers a fascinating glimpse of Fiji's multicultural community. The best times to visit are Friday and Saturday mornings, but the markets may sometimes be crowded to the point where it is difficult to walk through. All the products of land, lagoon and ocean are on display here, but avoid 'sword sellers' (see page 21) and 'guides' who will offer to take you to places where you will get the 'best deal.'

Return by following Stinson Parade south along the foreshore. At the junction with Central Street you'll find the **Curio & Handicraft Centre** ❹ (Stinson Road; tel: 331 3433; http://suvacity.org/curio-handicraft; Mon–Sat 8am–5pm), which sells a wide range of Fijian handicrafts, including replicas of old weapons, bowls, baskets, and *masi* (bark) items. While you may not find the cheapest souvenirs here, and there is no guarantee that absolutely everything has been made

individually by a craftsman, there's a good selection to browse through.

After you're all shopped out, keep going south along Stinson Parade, past Ratu Sukuna Park and eventually back to Victoria Parade. For dinner, try one of Fiji's finest Indian restaurants, **Ashiyana**, see ❷.

Food and drink

❶ BAD DOG CAFÉ

Corner Macarthur Street & Victoria Parade; tel: 331 2884; Mon–Thu 11am–11pm, Fri–Sat 11am–midnight; $$

Located right beside Suva's infamous O'Reilly's bar and nightclub, Bad Dog is the perfect place to pop in for a quick feed during a city gallivant, or to load up on fuel before a few drinks. The pizzas are popular, but you can choose from a selection of non-pretentious platters, including Mexican food or a simple Chicken Burger and chips.

❷ ASHIYANA

Old Town Hall, Victoria Parade; tel: 331 3000; www.ashiyanafiji.com; Mon–Sat 11.30am–2.30pm and 6–10pm, Sun 6–9.30pm; $$

Don't miss the chance to dine in one of Fiji's most fabulous Indian eateries, which specialises in South Indian dishes and Tandoori curries. If you're not sure, keep it simple and go for a classic like Roghan Josh. Prices are reasonable, but be aware you need to order rice and extras separately.

The Nausori Highlands frame the sugar cane fields

NAUSORI HIGHLANDS

Hire a four-wheel drive, prepare a picnic lunch, pack some swimming gear and set off to explore some of Fiji's inland wilderness. There are two routes to choose from, each with breathtaking and rugged scenery.

DISTANCE: Route 1: 90 miles (144km); route 2: 105 miles (166km)
TIME: A full day (for each option)
START/END: Nadi
POINTS TO NOTE: Do not attempt both itineraries on the same day. Whichever one you choose, make an early start for a full day of adventure. Allow at least 5 hours for each trip, plus extra time for swimming, picnicking and photography. Take food and water and don't expect to find anywhere to resupply en route. These are tours for the experienced driver as the roads can be somewhat treacherous, especially in the wet. Check conditions before setting out. Car rental companies will often insist on an indemnity clause for your four-wheel drive vehicle, as some cars have been damaged through careless or incompetent driving. Traditional villages in the highlands will not appreciate visits on a Sunday, which is the day of rest.

Leave the lazy beach life behind for a day or two, to go exploring along the coast and into the highland hills of the hinterland, where you can experience genuine village hospitality during a real tropical adventure.

ROUTE 1 – NAVALA AND BA

The distances involved are not great but because of road conditions, this route – with a stop for a swim and picnic, and a visit to Navala village – will require a whole day. Allow 15 minutes from Nadi to the Nausori Highlands road turn-off. The easiest way is to drive south (towards Suva) through town and turn left onto Nadi Back Road (there's a Hindu temple on the opposite side of the road). Follow this road for 3 miles (5km), keeping your eyes peeled for the Nausori Highlands signpost on your right. Take this road and follow it 21 miles (34km), to the Bukuya turn-off.

The road leaves the Nadi flats and begins ascending over an undulating landscape sprinkled with sugarcane farms towards the highlands, before turning steeply uphill and following a narrow ridge with sharp bends. Massive volcanic rocks and sheer cliff faces overlook-

A Navala bure

ing Nadi town, the airport and offshore islands offer good photo opportunities.

The road leaves the plantations and continues up steep terrain, threading through rainforest. On your right is the beginning of the Sigatoka River catchment, while to the left runs Nadi River. A turn-off to the left marks the access road to Vaturu Dam, the source of fresh water for Nadi and Lautoka.

If you want a less adventurous trip, turn left to the dam and, after a picnic lunch, return to Nadi by descending via the Sabeto Valley to the main highway north of the airport. Otherwise, continue on towards Bukuya for another 7 miles (12km) and turn left before reaching the village. The road now follows the Ba River catchment towards the village of Navala, 10 miles (17km) from the junction. On the way there are plenty of picturesque spots to stop for a picnic.

Navala

A genuinely traditional village with thatched *bures*, photogenic **Navala** ❶ provides an amazing cultural experience, but you must observe the correct etiquette. Don't turn up on a Sunday, don't wear a hat and, when you arrive, ask the first people you meet for directions to the chief. Fijian courtesy requires visitors to request permission to look around and take photographs, and this should be accompanied by a gift of F$15 and 1kg (2lb) of *yaqona* (the mildly narcotic powdered root of the piper mysthisticum plant) to the *turaga lli koro* (village headman).

To stay near the village, and visit with a local who can look after all the necessary polite procedures, try contacting Tui at **Bulou's Eco-Lodge** (Nav-

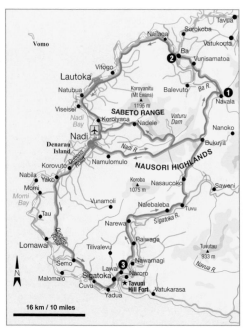

16 km / 10 miles

Interior of a bure in Navala

ala Village Road; tel: 628 1224/907 1722; email: sipirianotui@gmail.com; www.facebook.com/BulousEcoLodge). Visits here will include food and usually a traditional *kava* ceremony. Make contact before you leave, and be aware that you might need to be tenacious to get a response. You may also be able to enjoy a cool dip in the river, and experience paddling a *biribiri* (bamboo raft).

Ba and back

Allow an hour for the 11-mile (18km) drive from Navala to the township of Ba. As you descend from Navala, the road passes sugarcane farms and the compounds of Indian farmers and their families. Some of the fields are perched on ledges, demonstrating the ingenuity of the farmers.

On leaving Navala, the Ba River enters a gorge, where whitewater rafting sometimes takes place. The road begins its descent to Ba from a high ridge overlooking the lowlands and the sparkling sea in the distance. Much like the road up to the Nausori Highlands, it is steep and winding until it reaches low ground. The road is tarred some miles before the township and passes by the sugar mill on the banks of the river.

Ba ❷ itself is a quaint one-street collection of shops. The road will swing to the right, parallel to the Ba River. On your right moments later is the Ba Civic Museum (Mon–Thu 10am–5pm, Sat 9am–2pm), a tidy little place detailing the area's cane farming history with a collection of old machinery and a steam train.

Drive in the same direction as before until you reach a T-junction and turn left to cross Ba River by the bridge. The western side of the river has some rather ostentatious houses built by prosperous Indian merchants.

It is now 44 miles (70km) from Ba to Nadi and 23 miles (37km) to Lautoka on the sealed Kings Road. Allow extra time during the sugarcane harvest season, when you may encounter slow-moving trucks carting cane to the mill. The section between Ba and Lautoka offers great views of sugarcane fields and pine tree plantations on steep hills, and in the distance, Bligh Water and the Yasawa Islands.

ROUTE 2 – SIGATOKA VALLEY AND LAWAI

An alternative adventure can be enjoyed by driving 48 miles (77km) south from Nadi, along the Queens Road to Sigatoka (see page 47 for more details on this route) and, from there, venturing up the Sigatoka Valley road. This will eventually bring you back to Nadi through the Nausori Highlands, along the outbound section of the first route, above.

There are many points of interest along the first part of this route, including the Sigatoka sand dunes and, on the other side of the river at Naroro, a historic Tavuni hillfort (an old Tongan battlement; see page 48).

Lawai pottery   *Along the hiking trail to Naihehe Caves*

Lawai

Unless you're visiting the fort, don't cross Sigatoka River. Instead, turn left up the valley road to the village of **Lawai ❸**, where pottery is still made in the time-honoured Fijian way. This is a great place to pick up a unique souvenir.

The fecundity of the Sigatoka River Valley has earned it the title of the 'salad bowl' of Fiji. Many vegetables thrive in the rich soils here, and a government agricultural research station, 4 miles (6km) from town, is constantly experimenting with new varieties and species. The road up the valley is not tarred and requires attentive driving. It follows the river for most of the way and climbs two steep ridges, offering magnificent scenery.

There are villages on the way and 21 miles (35km) up the road, tobacco-drying kilns are a distinct landmark at Nalebaleba. About 4 miles (7km) further, after passing through Tuvu, take the road leading left to Bukuya. There are two villages on the way, both with access roads. The first is Nasaucoko village, headquarters of government troops during the little-talked-about 1876 Colo War, which occurred two years after the cession of Fiji to Britain, when a group of mountain people led by the Colo tribe began resisting colonial rule. It was here that some of the rebel leaders were hanged and the war was brought to an end.

It's just over 10 miles (17km) from the time you leave the valley road to the village of Bukuya. A little way past the village, take the turn to the left, which leads you back to Nadi.

Naihehe Caves

The extensive Naihehe Caves in the upper Sigatoka River Valley are remarkable. Originally formed by the sea, they're now found in a mountain of marble more than 30 miles (48km) from the ocean. These caves were used as a fortress during battles in Fiji's past. Regular tours to the Naihehe Caves are organised through Off Road Cave Safari (www.offroadfiji.com). These include a knowledgeable guide who will explain the history of the valley, especially its relation to a settlement of Tongan warriors. Typically there's a traditional *yaqona* welcome ceremony at the village, a tour of the caves, a ride downriver on a bilibili bamboo raft and a picnic lunch at the village. The caves were last used as a refuge and fortress in the 1875–76 Colo Wars. Today, the family of the Na Bete (priest) are the guardians and guides of the caves. The approach is via a beautiful walkway through a forest. A stream marks the entrance, where you must stoop low to get in. Once you enter, the cave opens into a series of huge chambers. The chambers have specific uses with the best parts reserved for the chief and the Na Bete. There are areas for sleeping, a maternity ward and a special place where human sacrifices were carried out and the flesh cooked.

LEVUKA: FIJI'S OLD CAPITAL

Levuka is a special place, frozen in time from the moment it was robbed of its title as a capital. Just getting there is an adventure, and those who venture beyond the tourist traps will be delightfully surprised with their discovery. This trip takes in all the major attractions, plus an interesting bush walk.

DISTANCE: 2 miles (3km)
TIME: A half day
START: Beach Street, Levuka
END: Levuka Village
POINTS TO NOTE: The easiest way to get to Levuka is to fly from Nausori Airport near Suva, to Ovalau's Bureta airstrip, and then catch a taxi or minibus to Levuka, which is on the other side of the island. The scenic 12-minute flight costs around F$90 one-way with Northern Air (tel: 347 5005/347 5003; www.northernair.com.fj; flights Mon–Sat). Alternatively, you can get a boat with Patterson Brothers' Shipping (tel: 331 5644; email: patterson@connect.com.fj; www.fijisearoad.com; sailing Mon–Sat), which operate a much cheaper 4-hour service to Ovalau, leaving from Suva City and stopping in Levuka Town.

Levuka – on the island of Ovalau, off the western coast of Viti Levu – is the former Fijian capital, and in 2013 it became the country's first World Heritage Site. Historically, it was important because of its position, close to the once-politically powerful states of Bau, Verata, Rewa and Cakaudrove, and the prevailing east-southeast trade winds allowed sailing ships to enter and leave the port without difficulty. Once Fiji became a British possession in 1874, however, Levuka's days as the country's capital were numbered, due to lack of available space. Still, it retains its appeal for inquisitive travellers, who enjoy the town's friendly ambience, sleepy colonial charm and the beauty of the surrounding area.

Levuka town, on Ovalau's southeast coast, sits on a narrow strip of land with a bush-clad mountain directly at its back. A stroll around the main sites and historic landmarks of the town could be done in an hour, but this is not a place for rushing around. Besides, there's only one flight and one boat arrival/departure most days, so you'll probably being staying at least one night.

BEACH STREET

Levuka's main (and only) thoroughfare, Beach Street, is one of the Pacific's

Locals in Levuka

best-preserved boulevards, and a veritable living museum of Fiji's colourful past. Most of the notable buildings are found along this road, grouped together around the harbour and Colonial Old Town. When you're in need of some sustenance, pop into **Whale's Tale**, see ❶.

That Levuka did not decline completely once it was dumped as the capital is partly due to a fish cannery operated by the Pacific Fishing Company, which employs most of the town. The PAFCO cannery is located next to the wharf at the southern end of Beach Street, and approximately half a mile south of this is **Nasova ❶** where a brace of anchors in a commemorative park mark the fact that this is where Fiji was ceded to Britain in 1874. It's also where, in 1970, Prince Charles (on behalf of Queen Elizabeth II) returned Fiji to the descendants of the chiefs who had given it to her great, great grandmother, Queen Victoria, 96 years previously.

Stroll north up Beach Street (note, there is no actual beach) and look out for a drinking fountain – this marks the site of Levuka's old **Pigeon Post ❷**, from where carrier pigeons once flew messages to and from Suva.

Of interest as you progress up Beach Street is the restored frontage of the 1868 **Morris Hedstrom** trading store, behind which is the charismatic little branch of the **Fiji Museum ❸** (Levuka Community Centre, Beach Street; Mon–Fri 8am–1pm and 2–4.30pm, Sat 9am–1pm).

Underlining the close connection of the sea and the influence of religion on every aspect of Fijian life, the Catholic **Sacred Heart Church ❹**, opposite the harbour, has a light on the bell tower that serves as a directional aid

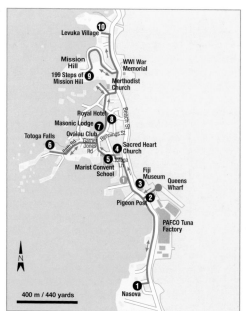

Levuka Village ⑩
Mission Hill
WWI War Memorial
199 Steps of Mission Hill ⑨
Methodist Church
Royal Hotel
Masonic Lodge ⑦ ⑧
Totoga Falls ⑥
Ovalau Club
Garner Jones Rd
Beach St
Hennings St
Sacred Heart Church ④
⑤
Marist Convent School
Totoga Ln
Fiji Museum ③
Queens Wharf
Pigeon Post ②
PAFCO Tuna Factory
N
Nasova ①
400 m / 440 yards

Boats moored up at Levuka

for approaching boats. It also has a quirky habit of chiming twice, once on the hour and once shortly afterwards.

BACK STREETS AND BUSHWALKING

Turn left just before the church, up Totoga Lane, to see the architecturally interesting **Marist Convent School ❺**, built out of coral stone (in an attempt to make it hurricane proof) in 1882.

Continue along Totoga Lane. When you reach Garner Jones Road, you can turn left and follow the road, which becomes Bath Road and goes past **Levuka Public School** (the oldest public school in Fiji, and educated many children who went on to become national leaders) before becoming a creekside track, climbing to the **Totoga Falls ❻** – where there are swimming holes (known as the Bath).

Retrace your steps to Garner Jones Road and follow this to a junction with Hennings Street. Turn left, cross Totoga Creek and go past the **Ovalau Club**

and the **Old Town Hall**, to check out the ruins of the **Masonic Lodge ❼**, Fiji's first when it was built in 1875. The club was torched by devout locals during the 2000 coup, apparently because of the masons' alleged links to the devil (a theory somewhat encouraged over the years by local Methodists). Further down, off to the right along Langham Street on the opposite side of the creek, is the **Royal Hotel ❽** (tel: 344 0024; www.royallevuka.com), which is the oldest operating hotel in the Pacific, partly dating from 1860.

MISSION HILL AND LEVUKA VILLAGE

Continue north along Chapel Street. On your right is a small war memorial to the town's inhabitants who died in WW1. Take the street heading inland across from it on your left, to the **Methodist Church** and the bottom of the **199 Steps of Mission Hill ❾**, which leads, unsurprisingly, to the top of Mission Hill (although, whoever named the steps couldn't count). Atop the hill stand several fine old buildings, including the **Delana Methodist School**.

Further north still, along Beach Street, past the hospital and the Church of the Holy Redeemer, you will find the traditional **Levuka Village ❿**, once home to Tui Levuka, the chief who first befriended early European settlers in Fiji, and a Methodist church where powerful Chief Cakobau worshipped in the 1870s, when he was finally converted to Christianity by tenacious missionaries.

Food and drink

❶ WHALE'S TALE

Beach Street; tel: 344 0235; Mon–Sat 9.30am–2pm, 5–9pm; $$

A laid-back, long-term Levuka favourite, which provides the perfect platform for a spot of people watching over a plate of prawns or sensational fish and chips.

Rafting the Navua River

NAVUA RIVER TRIP

Take an adventure-packed boat journey up the Navua River,
followed by a traditional welcome and lunch at Namuamua Village.

DISTANCE: 25 miles (40km) by boat
TIME: A full day
START/END: Navua
POINTS TO NOTE: While it might be possible to arrange an independent trip up the Navua River on a village punt by approaching boats directly, it's a lot easier to go with a reputable tour company such as Great Sights Fiji (tel: 672 3311; www.touristtransportfiji. com/great-sights-fiji), a division of Tourist Transport Fiji that has been delivering guided inland adventures in Fiji for years.

Navua is only 20 minutes from Suva, and if you're approaching from Nadi (as most people will be) the trip along Queen's Road offers spectacular views that delight with the ever-changing colours of the lagoon glimpsed through tall coconut trees. But the drive, pleasant as it is, is only an appetizer for the main course: the boat ride up the Navua river to Namuamua village.

NAVUA

The town of **Navua** ❶, which serves the farmers of the river delta, is small and rather slow, with buildings reminiscent of an earlier age and a marketplace that spills over the footpath and the edge of the road.

Although there is not a fantastic amount to do in Navua, and no real restaurants to explore for a pre-adventure feed (if you are looking for something substantial to line your stomach, you're better off stopping in Pacific Harbour en route), the produce market is the major focal point of the town and a really interesting place to stroll around. Markets such as this one are generally good spots to strike up a conversation with a local, and to taste some tropical fruits freshly picked from the tree.

Among the many flat-bottom, narrow punts at the town's river jetty are those that come to bring produce to the market every morning, which will return upriver later in the day. One of these will also take visitors to Namuamua village.

Punting up the river

RIVER RUNNING

Seated two abreast, hip-to-hip, your boat will have only a few inches of free-board. As the pilot cranks the outboard engine and your guide sits forward, the voyage will begin. About 40 minutes after leaving Navua, the punt will pass by **Nakavu ➋**, the last village with a road access. The river then enters a gorge, flanked by bush-clad hills. Look closely and you will see tall tree ferns, vine-clad tree trunks, clumps of bright green, fluffy bamboo and small grassy banks.

The river narrows and the punt, like a homing salmon, will find the line of least resistance up frothing rapids. Keep your eyes peeled for spectacular waterfalls as they tumble down cliff faces, some flashing like silver behind a screen of bamboo, others majestic as they gush 98ft (30 metres) into the river.

NUKUSERE

It takes another 40 minutes to reach Namua-mua village, but this can vary, depending on the engine size and the amount of water in the river. If the water level is low, the punt will require manhandling over the shallows, a function performed by the boatmen while you sit tight. The calm stillness of the river suggests unplumbed depths, but often the helmsman just leaps out, tilts the engine up and walks the punt over a shallow bank. As the punt emerges from the gorge, the country opens up gradually.

Nukusere ➌, high on the bank, is the first major village easily noticed because of the clutch of colourful

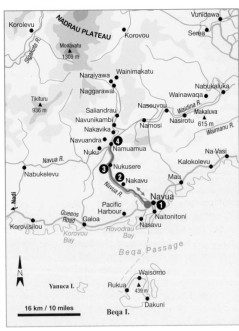

Experience a world-renowned shark dive

river punts moored below. The village was rebuilt on higher ground following a devastating cyclone and flood in 1982 washed away the original settlement, 10m (32ft) below where it now stands.

NAMUAMUA

A few hundred metres ahead, on the opposite bank, is the village of Namuamua. School children awaiting your arrival at the riverbank will lead you up into a house where a presentation of *yaqona* is made on your behalf (if you have arrived with a guide – if you're travelling independently you will need to source some *yaqona* to give to the chief and village people).

Once the *yaqona* is served, the guide takes the group on a tour of the village of **Namuamua ④**. After a hearty lunch of chicken, sausages, dalo leaves in coconut cream and boiled cassava, eaten on mats covering the floor, there is usually a *meke* (traditional dance) put on by a group of young men. The formal entertainment complete, the band will strike up a tune and invite you to dance.

Leaving the village mid-afternoon, you will get back to Navua town by about 4pm, as the trip on the punt downriver takes much less time. If you're with a guide, you should get the chance to enjoy paddling a *bilibili* (bamboo raft) and swimming in waterfall plunge pools on the way back.

Beqa Island

Navua is the port of departure for the volcanic island of Beqa, 7 miles (11km) offshore. This car-free paradise is a great spot for hiking, diving, surfing and getting to know Fijian people on their own turf. This is the traditional home of Fiji's legendary firewalkers, who originate from the village of Rukua. The gift of being able to walk on fire is said to have been bestowed on the men of the island 500 years ago by an eel, in exchange for its life. The island's barrier reef incorporates several beautiful islets within its lagoon, and the reef has a number of passages, including Frigate Passage, popular with surfers, and well known for magnificent left-hand waves. Beqa also has renowned coral reefs, ideal for snorkelling and diving. The brave can do a world-renowned shark dive – with bull sharks, and even the occasional tiger, and not a cage in sight – with Beqa Adventure Divers (www.fijisharkdive.com) on the appropriately named Shark Reef Marine Reserve. There are two resorts on the island – Beqa Lagoon Resort (www.beqalagoonresort.com) and Lalati Resort (www.lalatifiji.com) – and other accommodation options, many of which can transport you from Navau. Otherwise you can hop on a local boat, which usually leave the mainland between noon and 2.30pm Monday–Saturday, and take 1.5–2 hours to make the crossing.

YASAWA ISLANDS

A series of paradisiacal punctuation points splashed across the great blue canvas of the South Pacific, in the Yasawa Group you can enjoy a tropical island experience while delving a little deeper into the real Fiji.

DISTANCE: Varies
TIME: 4 days plus
START/END: Denarau
POINTS TO NOTE: There are several ways you can explore the islands of the Yasawa Group. You can splurge on a berth aboard one of the luxury vessels that float around the islands run by companies such as Blue Lagoon (www.bluelagooncruises.com), but those with an independent explorers' outlook will enjoy hitching a ride on the Awesome Adventures Fiji-operated Yasawa Flyer (www.awesomefiji.com), a passenger-carrying catamaran that ferries travellers up and down the archipelago. You can choose from a range of options (some of which cover accommodation too) from single-destination tickets to the multi-day Bula Pass, which allows you to island-hop freely. Accommodation across the islands takes the form of lodges and resorts – rated via a coconut-based grading system (three coconuts being the best) – and many of these resorts are village-owned and run.

While thousands of travellers annually flock to the Mamanuca Islands to enjoy neatly packaged, carefree, beach-based vacations with the occasional cultural theme, the slightly further flung Yasawa Group offers the chance to explore a far less predictable, wilder side of Fiji.

Here, besides enjoying sensational beaches, awesome aquatic adventures (including world-class snorkelling and diving) and all the rejuvenating delights of somnambulant island life, you can also experience a genuine cultural exchange with the locals, for example by attending church services and watching rugby games. Those particularly interested in learning about the realities of life in modern Fiji should explore the Vinaka Fiji programme (see box), which sees volunteers donate their time and expertise to help raise the standard of living, health and education of the local population.

The first European to sight the Yasawas was Captain Bligh, who sailed past the islands in a small boat in 1789, having just been cast adrift by his mutinous crew on board the *Bounty*, led by Fletcher Christian. Land-based tourism

The famous Blue Lagoon on Nanuya Lailai Island

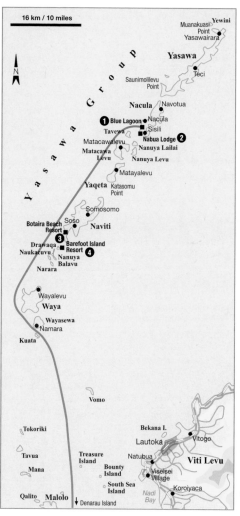

was forbidden on the Yasawa Islands until 1987, and many areas within this group retain a really remote, castaway feel.

The Yasawas' popularity is growing, however. At last count there were 22 resorts and lodges scattered across the 20 islands of the group, offering a wide range of beach-based accommodation and facilities – from the luxurious to the very basic. Many of these are village owned and run, and because the islands are bigger and properly populated, there's plenty of independent exploring to be done.

BLUE LAGOON

The outside world first became aware of the islands via Hollywood, through *Blue Lagoon*, a fictional story about two shipwrecked children stranded on a tropical island. The original film, with Jean Simmons, was released in 1949, but it was remade in 1980, controversially starring Brooke Shields, who was

Village children on Turtle Island

only 14 at the time. Both movies were shot on location in the Yasawa Group.

The islands' most famous feature is the real **Blue Lagoon ❶**, a much-celebrated pool on Nanuya Lailai, where utterly translucent water is fringed by almost impossibly fine-sanded beaches. Several resorts surround this dream-like lagoon, including the fancy 3-coconut-rated **Nanuya Island Resort** (tel: 666 7633; www.nanuyafiji.com), complete with treehouse *bures*. There are more budget-friendly options too, and other resorts operate boat trips to the lagoon so their guests can experience swimming and snorkelling in its idyllic embrace.

ISLAND-HOPPING

Several companies offer multi-day cruises departing from the ports of Denarau and Lautoka, and stopping at various islands in the chain, including **Captain Cook Cruises** (tel: 670 1823; www.captaincookcruisesfiji.com) and **Blue Lagoon Cruises** (tel: 670 5006; www.bluelagooncruises.com). However, as with the Mamanuca Group, the choice option for independent travellers looking to explore the islands at will is to travel on the *Yasawa Flyer*, operated by **Awesome Adventures Fiji** (tel: 675 0499; www.awesomefiji.com).

Leaving daily from Denarau, the *Yasawa Flyer* sails across the waves of the South Pacific and into Bligh Waters, weaving a magical route through the islands as far as the Blue Lagoon, stopping opposite all 22 resorts, from where little boats come out to collect and drop off guests. Single- and multi-day ticket options make it possible to spend your whole trip getting to know just one island, or to hop around and explore several.

The following itinerary is just one example of how you might spend a wonderful week experiencing the diversity of Yasawas, doing daytime trips to villages and sensational snorkelling spots, and spending long, balmy evenings dancing on the sand, after seeing the sun go down with a drink in your hand. Don't miss the opportunity to taste traditional feasts cooked in *lovos* (underground ovens) and to take part in kava ceremonies.

Nacula Island

Leaving from Denarau, stay on the *Yasawa Flyer* almost to the end of its daily journey – scoring a tantalising look at all the islands and resorts as you sail through – and hop off near the top of the archipelago, on Nacula Island, to spend a couple of days at **Nabua Lodge ❷**. The bures are basic at this one-coconut resort, but the friendly resort staff provide boat trips to the Blue Lagoon, where you can enjoy (probably) the most sensational beach experience of your life, with absolutely no crowds. Other trips from here include one to Nacula Cave, where you explore fascinating limestone caverns, including one that's only accessible via a leap of faith and a very dark swim through an underwater tunnel.

An exquisite Yasawa sunset

Floating cocktails at Turtle Island

Naviti Island

When you're ready to go, jump back on the Yasawa Flyer as far as **Botaira Beach Resort ❸** (http://botaira.com), a three-coconut joint on Naviti Island. There are also many trips available from this family friendly resort, but with world-class reef snorkelling available a mere 10 metres (33ft) from the door of your beachfront *bure*, you might not want to travel anywhere else for several days. Enjoy relaxing on the beach, cooling down with an occasional plunge into the kaleidoscopically-colourful world beneath the water, where myriad fantastic fish and soft corals compete for your attention in a non-stop natural show.

Drawaqwa Island

Board the Yasawa Flyer again to scoot around to **Barefoot Island Resort ❹** (https://barefootmantafiji.com) on Drawaqwa Island. This is the place to get adventurous. The island has its own dive shop, run by the excellent Australian-owned, locally staffed company **Reef Safari** (www.reefsafari.com/fiji), and there are dozens of world-class diving sites to be explored, including many wrecks. Non-divers can snorkel and swim with giant manta rays just off the beach (the enormous animals swim through the channel between Drawaqwa and its neighbouring island almost daily), and there's also the opportunity to go night snorkelling, abseiling, trekking, and sea kayaking. The bar is lively most nights, and the company is entertaining, whether you're hanging out with locals and sipping *kava* as the sun goes down, or trying your hand at Fiji Bitter-fuelled coconut bowling with a bunch of Scandinavian backpackers.

Vinaka Fiji

Fiji feels like paradise to visitors, but despite their seemingly perpetual upbeat appearance, life isn't always easy for the local populace. There are 27 villages sprinkled through the Yasawa Island chain, and they all exist below the poverty line. Vinaka Fiji is a voluntourism project based in the Yasawas, which welcomes participation from visitors, whether you're intending to spend a few days or several months on the islands. Paying volunteers receive accommodation at Barefoot Island Resort while taking part in a series of social and eco-orientated projects, designed to help raise the standard of living, health and education of the local people, and to protect the fragile environment. The options are numerous, ranging from roles in village schools and mother-and-baby clinics, through to baby clam-cleaning duties for scuba divers (clams help destroy the eggs of the reviled crown-of-thorns starfish, a highly invasive species that reproduces at a frightening rate and sucks the life out of the reef). Volunteering programs (inclusive of accommodation at Barefoot Island Resort) can be arranged through Vinaka Fiji www.vinakafiji.org.fj.

Waitatavi Bay, Vanua Levu

EXPLORING FIJI'S NORTH

For those who like to venture off the beaten track, Fiji's north offers rich rewards in the shape of interesting islands, fascinating villages and world-class diving. Take a scenic drive with lots of local flavour.

DISTANCE: 14 miles (22km) by ferry and 80 miles (128km) by road
TIME: A full week
START: Savusavu
END: Bouma National Heritage Park
POINTS TO NOTE: Ideally, allow a few days to get the most out of this route, staying at resorts and islands along the way. The fastest way to get to the start is to fly to Savusavu; Fiji Airways (www.fijiairways.com) operate regular flights from Nadi and Suva (Nausori) to Savusavu. Another option is to sail between the islands; Fiji Searoad Service (www.fijisearoad.com) run a ferry service between Viti Levu's Suva (Mon–Sat) or Lautoka (Mon, Wed and Fri) and Savusavu. To explore at your own pace, you will need to rent a car, but there is a daily bus service between Savusavu and Natuvu, which arrives in time to connect with a small ferry for the 2-hour trip to Waiyevo on the island of Taveuni. From the end, you can retrace your steps or fly directly back to Nadi or Suva from Matei Airport on Taveuni.

In Fiji, the 'north' is a general term applied to the islands of Vanua Levu, Taveuni, Qamea, Laucala, Rabi, Kioa, Matagi and the magical Ringold Isles, as well as the coral reefs of Heemskirk, Qele-levu, Wailangilala and Duff. The largest of these islands is Vanua Levu, which, at 2,137 sq miles (5,535 sq km) is about half the size of Viti Levu. Vanua Levu is irregular in shape, running on a south-west to northeast axis for approximately 100 miles (160km) and seldom exceeding 30 miles (48km) in width. As on Viti Levu, a mountainous interior runs the length of the island. The highlands are closer to the east coast, where they trap the moisture-laden southeast trade winds, creating an effect that divides the island climatically, with the east receiving much more rain than the west. Sugarcane is grown on the western side and Labasa, which grew up around the sugar mill, rivals Lautoka as Fiji's second city.

SAVUSAVU

Strategically positioned halfway along the east coast of Vanua Levu, the town-

The Nai'a Flaya dive in the Bligh Water area between Vanua Levu and Viti Levu

ship of **Savusavu** ❶ nestles around one of the most beautiful natural harbours in the Pacific, and is one of Fiji's major ports. The commercial centre of Savusavu hugs a narrow coastal strip beside the harbour. Nawi Island is immediately offshore and the deep water between the island and the town is a perfect anchorage for visiting yachts. Near the wharf are some hot springs, a reminder that Savusavu Bay was once a volcanic caldera.

If you're staying the night in Savusavu, or want to fuel up before leaving town, check out **Surf 'n' Turf**, see ❶.

Savusavu boasts some spectacular dive sites, located at the entrance to Savusavu Bay and along the coast leading to Taveuni. The road leading east out of town follows the bay to **Lesiaceva Point** ❷. There are a number of hotels and resorts on this stretch, including the upmarket **Jean-Michel Cousteau Resort Fiji** (www.fijiresort.com) and, over the hill and a bit further east along the coast, **Namale Resort** (www.namalefiji.com) (see page 83).

HIBISCUS HIGHWAY

It's a good 40 miles (64km) from Savusavu along the scenic Hibiscus Highway to Buca Bay. For an alternative adventure, you can turn left 2 miles (3km) past Koro Sun Resort, and go northeast around Natewa Bay for 81 miles (130km), crossing the mountains and eventually reaching **Labasa**, the largest town in Vanua Levu.

To follow our route, however, continue along the highway until you reach the Natuvu turnoff for the ferry to Taveuni, which leaves from **Buca Bay** ❸. Two islands sit just offshore here – Rabi and Kioa – home to very different communities. Following WWII, the British rehoused the people of Banaba Island (part of the Republic of Kiribati) on Rabi, after their homeland was rendered largely uninhabitable by phosphate mining. Kioa, however, was purchased on behalf of the people of Tuvalu, who were given the island in recognition of their work with the US armed forces during the war, mostly against Japanese forces.

TAVEUNI

The ferry to Taveuni runs daily and takes two hours to arrive at **Waiyevo** ❹. As well as being Fiji's third largest landmass, Taveuni is the country's youngest island (geologically speaking). It's of volcanic origin and is known as the 'garden isle' because of its rich soils and luxuriant vegetation, which includes large tracts of rainforest and a profusion of bird life. The 180th meridian of longitude passes through the island, running slightly west of Waiyevo, and in theory, it's possible to straddle this line so one of your feet will be in the 'today' zone and the other in 'yesterday'. However, for purposes of keeping Fiji in the same time zone, this distinction is often ignored.

Soon after crossing the dateline, you reach the settlement of **Wairiki** ❺,

Wairiki Catholic Church

dominated by a large Catholic church and a cross on the hill above it. The spot marks the scene of a crucial battle, where the hitherto undefeated forces of the Tongan chief Ma'afu suffered a decisive loss against the locals led by the Tui Cakau (Lord of the Reef).

It's 20km (12.4 miles) from Waiyevo to **Vuna** ❻, at the southern end of the island, and an additional 7km (4 miles) to **South Cape** ❼. The drive northeast from Waiyevo is equally spectacular, with the road passing the settlement and vil-

lage of **Somosomo** ❽, seat of the Tui Cakau, paramount chief of the province of Cakaudrove. A former incumbent, Ratu Sir Penaia Ganilau, was Fiji's last Governor-General and first President.

The drive continues along the coast to Naselesele Point and the airport at Matei. There are several places offering accommodation here, and if you're peckish, check out the **Coconut Grove**, see ❷. Follow the road as it then bears southeast to reveal a colourful lagoon dotted with small islets and the bigger

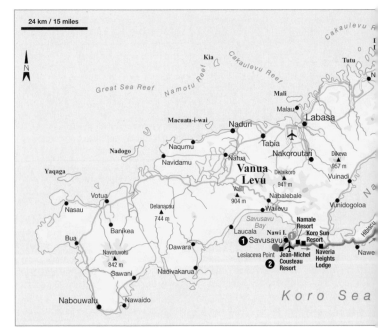

Villa at the Laucala Island Resort

islands of Qamea and Laucala. **Navakacoa landing** ❾, about 5 miles (8km) from the airport, is the pickup point for the islands of Qamea, Laucala and Matagi. Each island has a resort-style hotel. Laucala, which was once the private playground of publishing tycoon Malcolm Forbes, has a small, exclusive resort with prices to match.

About 7km (4 miles) from Navakacoa landing, you'll discover the **Tavoro Waterfall** ❿ on the outskirts of **Bouma National Heritage Park**. There is a nom-inal admission fee and it's a 5-minute walk to the waterfall, one of the most spectacular in Fiji. A large volume of water plunges from over 70ft (22 metres) down into a pool surrounded by lush rainforest. If you have time, a cool, refreshing swim and picnic (barbecue facilities available on site) are highly recommended.

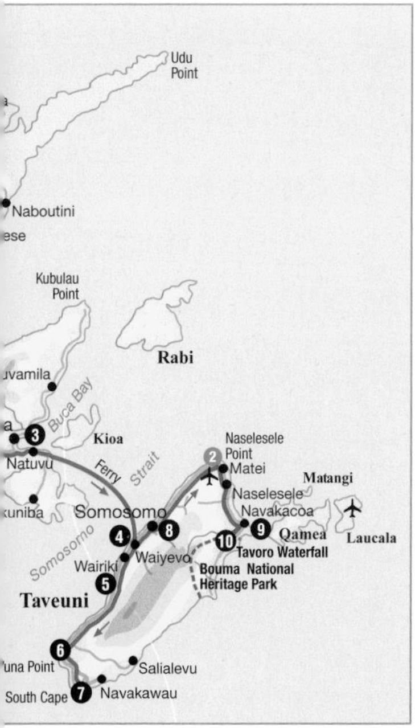

Food and drink

❶ SURF 'N' TURF

Savusavu, Vanua Levu; tel: 885 3033; Mon–Sat 10am–9.30pm; $$

Not the cheapest joint in town, but a restaurant where the quality of the local seafood and imported steak is simply superb. Try the slipper lobster or, even better, the Kokonda – a raw fish salad that is a speciality of the chef, who spent over 10 years preparing grommet dishes at Jean-Michel Cousteau's swanky resort around the corner on the coastal road.

❷ COCONUT GROVE RESTAURANT

Coconut Grove Beachfront Cottages, Taveuni Island; tel: 888 0328; www. coconutgrovefiji.com/restaurant; $$$

Offering a mouth-watering menu mix of traditional South Pacific island classics and spicy Indian curries, this place reflects the contemporary cultural complexion of Fiji in delicious fashion. Fish and other seafood are always fantastic options here, but it's all good, from the homemade pasta to the home-grown greens.

(Map showing Taveuni and surrounding islands with labels: Udu Point, Naboutini, Kubulau Point, Rabi, Juvamila, Buca Bay, Kioa, Naselesele Point, Matei, Matangi, Naselesele, Navakacoa, Qamea, Laucala, Natuvu, Somosomo, Ferry Strait, ❸, ❹, ❽, ❿, ❾, Wairiki, Waiyevo, Tavoro Waterfall, Bouma National Heritage Park, Taveuni, ❺, ❻, una Point, Salialevu, South Cape, ❼, Navakawau, kuniba)

DIRECTORY

Hand-picked hotels and restaurants to suit all budgets and tastes, organised by area, plus select nightlife listings, an alphabetical listing of practical information, a language guide and an overview of the best books and films to give you a flavour of the islands.

Entrance to the Novotel Nadi

ACCOMMODATION

Fiji is a destination that caters well for a diverse range of visitors, from footloose international wanders, travelling through the tropics on a shoestring, to the honeymooners and baby boomers who arrive with high expectations and cash to splash on accommodation that they then won't stray too far away from. The eclectic nature of the crowds that come through Nadi's international airport have obviously shaped the country's accommodation offerings, especially within the archipelagos that scatter off into the ocean to the northwest of Viti Levu, where resorts can vary enormously even though they might only be a few hundred metres away from one another, on the other side of a small island, across a lagoon or a narrow channel of water.

Some are very backpacker-friendly, with a few basic *bures* and a bar, while others are ultra glitzy, pimped out to the max, with super luxurious resorts built amid the coconut trees, and complete with private plunge pools and king-size four-poster beds. Helpfully, in the absence of any official rating system, Awesome Adventures Fiji, the company that operate a ferry service to many of these islands, have dreamed up a coconut grading system for resorts in the Mamanuca and Yasawa island groups – which assigns between one and three coconuts to lodges and resorts the boat services, to give people some idea of what to expect. One coconut means conditions are quite basic, three means the resort is quite swish – beyond that, for the really fancy places, most people will be arriving by float plane, yacht or a resort-run private boat.

On the bigger islands and in the cities, price is the only real indicator, although it would be fair to say that the most expensive is not necessarily the best. On arrival at Nadi International Airport and after immigration formalities, you will see a listing of various accommodation options with published rates. Fiji Tourism officials at the airport will help those who have not made prior bookings. Better deals are almost certainly out there to be found online, where you can often find reduced rates. There is no high or low season for room rates in Fiji, though sometimes specials are offered during the off-season months of February and March. The following symbols indicate price ranges for

---

Price for a double room/*bure* for one night:
$$$$ = over F$500
$$$ = F$250–500
$$ = F$100–250
$ = below F$100

A room at the DoubleTree Resort by Hilton

a double standard room or a *bure* in an island resort (where food is almost always included, even at the cheaper end of the scale). Note that all prices are subject to a hefty government tax of 25 percent, which is normally rolled into the overall price, however it is always helpful to double check before committing to a reservation.

Nadi area

DoubleTree Resort by Hilton

Sonaisali Island; tel: 670 6011; https://doubletree3.hilton.com; $$$

Sonaisali is an island resort, 20-minutes from Nadi airport, with a range of accommodation and entertainment options. It has a good pool, complete with a bar. As a whole, it leans heavily towards the honeymoon market. Rooms are comfortable, although the cost of a round-trip to Nadi is quite high.

Novotel Nadi

Namaka Hill; tel: 672 2000; www.accorhotels.com; $$$

Located near the airport and just 15 minutes from Port Denarau for boat transfers to the islands, there's no question that this place is convenient, and the staff are friendly and helpful. The hotel luxuriates in 42 acres of tropical gardens, and all rooms have a view of the golf course. Rooms are slightly dated for the price tag, however.

Raffles Gateway Hotel

Queens Road; tel: 673 4755; www.fijigateway.com; $$$

Found 5 miles (8km) from the centre of town, Raffles is right opposite the entrance to the Nadi International Airport, making it most convenient for transfers, and there's a handy 24-hour courtesy bus to the airport. Rooms are pleasant, although they don't come with many extras. The pool – complete with a great slide – is a hit with the kids.

Sheraton Fiji Resort

Denarau Island; tel: 675 0777; www.sheratonfiji.com; $$$$

Positioned on Denarau Island, this modern Mediterranean-style resort has 297 rooms with balconies overlooking both garden and sea, plus 6 swimming pools, 14 eating and drinking areas and an adjoining 18-hole golf course. Room rates include a buffet breakfast and complimentary non-motorised water sports. It's well-run, with friendly staff.

Coral Coast

The Crow's Nest

Queens Highway, Korotogo; tel: 650 0230; www.crowsnestresortfiji.com; $$

Featuring private cottages and bures neatly located on the side of a hill overlooking the lagoon and ocean, this place has undergone a major refurb, and the results have been pleasing guests ever since. The fare served in the restaurant is consistently superb. Staff are excellent too.

Room at the Outrigger Fiji Beach Resort

Hideaway Resort

Queens Road, Sigatoka; tel: 650 0177; www.hideawayfiji.com; $$$

On a beach in the Korolevu area, this is a fun place with a well-known surfbreak just beyond the reef. Accommodation is right by the seashore in cottages and ocean-front *bures* set among coconut palms and flowering shrubs. There's an attractive pool with water slide.

InterContinental Fiji Golf Resort & Spa

Maro road, Natadola Bay; tel: 673 3300; www.ihg.com; $$$$

Right next to one of Fiji's most spectacular beaches, this luxury resort has suites and classic rooms, various restaurants and bars and plenty of water sports offered on site. However the major draw of this location for many is the 18-hole PGA-endorsed golf course.

The Naviti

Queens Highway, Korolevu; tel: 653 0444; www.warwickhotels.com/naviti-resort; $$$

A pleasant retreat with nice beach, pool and even a small island nearby. The full range of activities are available, including snorkelling and kayaking. There's a kids' club and entertainment is staged nightly. Staff are helpful and all-inclusive packages are available.

Outrigger Reef Fiji Resort

Sigatoka; tel: 650 0044; www.outrigger. com; $$$

A very family friendly option, offering a mix of accommodation, including beautiful bures with spectacular views. Features include a fabulous 'Vahavu' tropical pool and a hilltop Bebe Spa. Meimei nannies are available, plus there's a range of activities for children and teens, and kids eat for free.

Shangri-La's Fijian Resort

Yanuca Island; tel 652 0155; www.shangri-la.com/fijianresort; $$$

There are more than 400 rooms at this Yanuca Island resort, which boasts an excellent beach, five restaurants, seven bars, a shopping arcade and a 9-hole golf course. You can arrange plenty of activities, including a half-day tour to a local school, plus snorkelling and canoeing.

Pacific Harbour/Beqa Island

Beqa Lagoon Resort

Beqa Island; tel: 330 4042; www. beqalagoonresort.com; $$$$

Arriving by boat, skimming across the cobalt blue Beqa Lagoon, is a pretty impressive way to start your stay, so the rest of the resort has a lot to live up to, which it proceeds to do. Accommodation is in *bures* set amongst the paradisiacal surrounds of a palm-tree covered island, perfect for divers but stunning for everyone. The resort has an infinity pool, while the *bures* feature private plunge pools, exotic koi ponds and beautiful ocean views. Kids welcome.

The pool at Shangri-La's Fijian Resort

The Pearl South Pacific Resort

Queens Road, Pacific Harbour; tel: 773 0022; www.thepearlsouthpacific.com; $$$

Another recently renovated resort that now lives up to its image as a super-swanky joint, complete with a swim-up bar, is the Pearl Spa. It also has an 18-hole championship golf course. Staff are fantastically attentive, and the rooms (especially those overlooking the harbour and islands) are highly recommended.

Suva

Five Princes Hotel

5 Princes Road; tel: 338 1575; www.fiveprinceshotel.com; $$$

A boutique bolthole that provides a fantastically friendly alternative to the big chain hotels typically found in Suva. Choose from 10 good-sized rooms in the main hotel, or bag a *bure* out in the green grounds (perfect if you're travelling as a family). Rooms come with tea and coffee making facilities, the hotel has a nice cool pool, and although it's on a main road, the only noise that you're likely to hear is singing from the church next door. The main attraction is the personal touch from the owner and staff. Food is also available.

Holiday Inn

501 Victoria Parade; tel: 330 1600; www.ihg.com/holidayinn/suva; $$$

A consistent performer in the capital, with excellent staff. Rooms come with high-speed internet and a balcony – try and get one with a sea or pool view. The location is handy for exploring downtown Suva, with all the sights and restaurants reachable within a short walk, including Thurston Gardens. There's a cool pool to dive into when the heat gets too much, and a good bar, plus several eating options to explore.

Novotel Suva Lami Bay

Queens Road, Lami Bay; tel: 336 2450; www.accorhotels.com; $$

A more affordable Suva option, albeit a little further out of town (15 minutes' drive). There are islands views from the rooms, and you can dine in-house by the waterfront, or sip a sundowner from the tropical bar. Service is not necessarily the fastest.

Mamanuca Islands

Beachcomber Island Resort

Beachcomber Island; tel: 666 1500 or 666 2600; www.beachcomberfiji.com; $$$

A tiny island, perpetually filled with fun-loving people. It caters to day-trippers too, but once the boats have left for the night the island belongs to backpackers and the young-at-heart. Entertainment is put on nightly, and there are myriad activities to enjoy. Accommodation ranges from dormitories to hotel rooms and private *bures*. Meals are typically included.

Malolo Island Resort

Malolo Island; tel: 672 0978; www.

Deluxe bure living at Toberua Island Resort

maloloisland.com; $$$

A resort fully owned by a Fijian family, Malolo offers a more rustic experience for those who want to feel like they're in the real Fiji, rather than a polished luxe version of the destination. The hospitality is sensational, and genuine, and the facilities are beautifully simple – a *bure* on the beach. Sand. Sea. Sun. Coral reefs and coconut palms – and no mod cons to interrupt you. Very family friendly.

Mana Island Resort

Mana Island; tel: 665 0423; www.manafiji.com; $$$

Sitting pretty on a 300-acre tropical island, fringed by white sandy beaches and gin-clear waters, this resort offers a spectrum of accommodation options, from *bures* to luxury suites, with prices ranging accordingly. Welcoming to everyone, from families to honeymooners. All the usual activities are available.

Matamanoa Island Resort

Matamanoa Island; tel: 672 3620; www.matamanoa.com; $$$$

An adults-only resort, which doesn't cater for day-trippers, Matamanoa Island is a refuge for couples looking for an intimate and secluded holiday on a tropical island. Accommodation options range from beachfront *bures* (complete with private plunge pools) and villas, to resort rooms. On top of the usual activities, there's an excellent tennis court on the island. The restaurant's a la carte dinner menu changes each day.

Musket Cove Resort

Malolo Lailai Island; tel: 666 2215; www.musketcovefiji.com; $$$$

Built by Australian entrepreneur and occasional adventure, Dick Smith, the so-called father of Mamanuca resorts, guests at Musket Cove have 400 acres of verdant hills and palm-fringed beaches to explore on Malolo Lailai Island, the only one in the group with an airstrip. Garden, lagoon and beachfront *bures* are available here, as well as island villas equipped with kitchenettes and ideal for larger groups and families.

Tavarua Island Resort

Tavarua Island; tel: 776 6513; www.tavarua.com; $$$$

A heart-shaped island, this place will get everyone all loved up, but especially surfers, as the island offers access to some of the best breaks in the world, including Fiji's most famous wave, Cloudbreak. Non-surfers are well catered for too in this intimate resort, with just 16 *bures*, all nicely positioned and with air-conditioning. Other adventures include sea kayaking and SUP paddling.

Outer islands

Toberua Island Resort

Toberua Island; tel: 992 9190; www.toberua.com; $$$$

Snorkelling outside a bure, Toberua Island Resort

There are 16 beachfront bures on this idyllic and private island, with three options: premium, deluxe or tropical. Activities here, when you're not barefoot dancing to Fijian tunes or lounging in a hammock, include playing golf on a unique 9-hole, low-tide golf course. You can also go snorkelling, kayaking and paddling on Hobie Cats and SUPs.

Wakaya Club

Wakaya; tel: 344 8128; www.wakaya.com; $$$$

The accommodation is palatial here. With each bure offering 1,650 sq ft (153 sq metres) of space, you'll feel like a chief. The space is used well too, with four-poster king size beds and oversized soaking tubs tailing up some of it. Outside you have killer ocean views, and there's a spa at your service. Rates are all inclusive, with booze and even a scuba dive thrown in for good measure (and the diving is particularly excellent).

Levuka Homestay

Church Street, Levuka; tel: 344 0777; www. levukahomestay.com; $$

The hospitality served up by hosts John and Marilyn is almost as legendary as the breakfast they dish out daily at this extremely welcoming homestay, situated between the village and the colonial old town. A proper home from home.

Royal Hotel

Beach Street, Levuka; tel: 344 0024; www. royallevuka.com; $$

In the country's historic former capital, Fiji's oldest working hotel is full of character and charm, and staffed by people who know how to make you feel at home. It provides everything you need, including a harbour view, and the price tag is extremely reasonable. You can get rooms from F$53 per double, but the options also stretch to garden apartments and private 3-bedroom cottages (a real bargain for F$150 per cottage per night).

Barefoot Island Resort

Drawaqwa Island; tel: 776 3040; www. barefootmantafiji.com; $$$

There are three beaches at this resort – one for watching the sunrise, one for sunset and one for swimming with gigantic manta rays that cruise through the channel between Drawaqwa and the neighbouring island on an almost daily basis during some parts of the year. There's an excellent dive school on site, with a boat that will take you to explore literally dozens of dive sites, and a fabulous coral garden sits just off the beach, perfect for snorkelling. The dive school operates a night snorkelling experience, which is fantastic, and you can even go abseiling. The Beachside bures are available as en suite or basic, depending on your budget, and there's entertainment every night. The Vinaka Fiji voluntourism project operates out

Jean-Michel Cousteau Fiji Resort private island trip

of here too. The Barefoot group also run Barefoot Kuata Island, another Yasawa gem, located on the Waya collection of islands and an excellent diving spot.

Botaira Resort

Naviti Island; tel: 603 0200; http://botaira.com; $$$$

An excellent value three-coconut resort, where the food is plentiful and all inclusive (as it is on most of the islands), served on a deck with stunning ocean views. From your comfortable beachside bure, you have to walk all of 5 or 10 metres to reach the super clear sea, where the snorkelling is absolutely sensational. There are also kayaks at your disposal, and it's possible to visit a local village church service.

Nabua Lodge

Nacula Island; tel: 925 5370; $$$

The Yasawa Islands are a place of glorious contrasts, and while some of the lodges are extremely luxurious and expensive, there are always affordable options, and this is the perfect example. Bures are simple, but more than adequate, and the hospitality is great at this budget-friendly resort, which also offers dorm accommodation. The food is good without being ridiculously flash, and while the local beach isn't mind blowing, you can do trips to the impossibly gorgeous Blue Lagoon and to Nacula Cave to explore semi submerged caves.

Turtle Island Fiji

Nanuya Levu; tel: (Australian number) +61 3 9823 8300; www.turtlefiji.com; $$$$

An almost outrageously luxurious resort on a private island, where you arrive by float plane to be met by singing staff on the beach, and wash down stunning seafood with Moët champagne during a beach picnic. Everything is inclusive, and the resort caters for just 14 couples at a time.

Vanua Levu

Jean-Michel Cousteau Fiji Resort

tel: (Au) 1300-306 171, (USA) 800-246 3454; www.fijiresort.com; $$$$

Built across 17 fecund acres of a former coconut plantation, the Jean-Michel Cousteau Fiji is a super luxury resort with 25 beautiful bures, each with private decks discreetly tucked away beneath flowing bougainvillea and gently swaying coconut trees. There's a spa in the resort, and a private island called Naviavia to which you can kayak, while the staff bring over a chilled bottle of champagne and a picnic.

Koro Sun Resort

Hibiscus Highway, near Savusavu; tel: 885 0262; www.korosunresort.com; $$$$

The accommodation options here include sumptuous treetop villas with outdoor showers quite literally in the foliage of trees, plus private plunge pools, day beds and a wet bar. There are several styles of bure, including those that 'float' on the Edgewater lagoon. The 160–acre sanctuary-style resort, built on an old plantation, also has a

golf course, swimming pool and tennis courts. It's 8 miles (13km) east of Savusavu.

Namale Resort

Hibiscus Highway, Savusavu; tel: 800-727 3454; www.namalefiji.com; $$$$

This resort, part of a former copra plantation, is tucked away on a small peninsula with a white sandy beach facing the lagoon and a deep bay on its right flank. An atmosphere of tranquillity is fostered through the lush landscaping and by limiting the number of guests to a maximum of 20 at any one time. Resort guests are accommodated in bures, featuring traditional thatch roofs, exquisite interiors and private decks with spectacular views. The resort also offers excellent scuba diving, as well as a full range of activities.

Naveria Heights Lodge

Naveria, Savusavu; tel: 885 0348; www.naveriaheightsfiji.com; $$$

There are three boutique-style guest rooms in this laid-back lodge, all with cracking views over the highlands, islands and ocean. Guests can also socialise in the communal areas, which include a Fijian style lounge and a tree-top plunge pool. Rates include local airport transfers and a healthy breakfast.

Taveuni

Garden Island Resort

Waiyevo, Taveuni Island; tel: 888 0286; www.gardenislandresort.com; $$$

Located on Fiji's third-largest island, this great green place is a fantastic find for anyone – with sensational sea-view suites and an awesome ocean-front spa – but it's scuba divers who will be smiling the most. There are more than 20 dive sites within 15 minutes of the Garden Island Resort, including the famous Rainbow Reef, a kaleidoscope of soft coral colour and saline action.

Matagi Island Resort

Matangi Island; tel: 778 0061; www.matangiisland.com; $$$$

This resort, with its distinct bures built on a hexagonal plan, is located on a 240-acre copra plantation on a little isle, some distance off Taveuni's north-east coast. Beside the bures, your accommodation options include a split-level treehouse, designed with honeymooners in mind, but available to anyone. Built beside a beautiful white-sand beach, it stares out across a blue lagoon at Qamea island. The family-run resort carefully limits its intake to 24 guests at any one time, and operates two live-aboard dive vessels, taking full advantage of some of the most superb diving and cruising in the world. The opposite side of the island has the famous Horse Shoe Bay and beach. There is a full programme of activities, including village tours and an excursion to the Bouma waterfalls on mainland Taveuni.

Sophisticated style at Ports O' Call

RESTAURANTS

Fiji's fantastic food scene is as colourful and varied as the diverse ethnic make-up the country's population would suggest, and on the streets and in markets, restaurants and resorts all around the islands, you will find cracking cuisine from the South Pacific, Asia (especially India) and Europe. Fans of seafood and spicy dishes are particularly well catered for, and if you like seafood curries, you may have just landed in your own personal paradise.

Apart from restaurants recommended in the itineraries, the following listings are some of the best places to eat around the islands. Typically, the best food is served at the best hotels and resorts. On the islands, food is usually included in the price of accommodation, and in the high-end resorts, the feasts laid on for top-paying guests can look like something prepared for Caligula.

However, there are also some gems to be found on the streets of Fiji's towns and cities – particularly those with a large Indo-Fijian presence. Many good hotel and resort restaurants will serve a range of Fijian, Indian, Chinese and European dishes as well as buffets and traditional *lovo* meals (see page 16).

Nadi

Chan's Seafood Restaurant

Lot 1, Northern Press Road, Martintar; tel: 921 6921; daily 11am–10pm; $$

Portions are generous at this great Chinese restaurant with a decent view. Try the steamed coconut crab for something a bit special, or go for the lobster. Service isn't always the fastest.

Curry House

Hospital Road, Nadi; tel: 670 0798; 11am–6pm; $$

The crab is recommended at this local chow joint, as are the prawn dishes. If you're on a budget, ignore the more expensive options such as the lobster, and go simple by ordering the chicken choosey – which is highly rated.

Daikoku Japanese Restaurant

Corner Northern Press Road and Queens Road, Martintar; tel: 670 3623; www. daikokufiji.com/fiji; Mon–Sat noon–2pm, 6–9.30pm; $$$

The sashimi is sublime at this highly regarded Japanese restaurant in

For the purposes of this book, we have used the following price guide, based on the average price for a two-course meal for one, with a drink.
$$$$ = above F$60
$$$ = F$40–60
$$ = F$20–$40
$ = F$20

Denarau. Teppanyaki is also on offer, individually prepared at your Teppan table, as well as standard classic Japanese cuisine such as sukiyaki, shabu shabu and so on. If you're bamboozled by the menu, ask the friendly waitstaff for some direction, or just dive into the Carnivore platter, starting with the aptly named Yum Yum prawns. The restaurant is very child friendly, but make a reservation, as they will fill up at busy times of the week.

Indigo Indian Asian Restaurant

Port Denarau Marina, Denarau Island; tel: 675 0026; www.indigofiji.com; daily 11am–10pm; $$$

Overlooking the port, this Indian-Asian fusion restaurant has been serving delicious curries and other dishes for some time now, and has become a favourite for visitors about to hit the islands. Kick things off with a classic Indian starter, such as samosas and bhajis, before moving on to the curries, which come in various styles, from Thai to Singaporian. The Szechuan dishes – splashed in Indigo's signature spicy sauce – hits the mark very nicely, as does the Fijian duck.

Ports O' Call

Sheraton Fiji Resort, Denarau Island; tel: 675 0777; Mon–Sat 6pm–10pm; $$$$

For over two decades this fancy French-influenced restaurant within the Denarau Sheraton, decked out to resemble the true luxury of a classic ocean liner, has been serving up fine fare. Treat yourself with an entrée of French Bouillabaisse with reef lobster, mud crab, prawns and walu fillet in an herb and saffron broth, followed by a steak Diane flambéed at your tableside, and round it off with a crêpes Suzette. Dress smart or be disappointed at the door.

Saffron Tandoori Restaurant

Jack's Mall Sagayam Road; tel: 670 3131; Mon–Sat 9am–5pm; $$

Providing an air-conditioned refuge from the mean street of Nadi after some souvenir shopping, this place offers a tasty selection of authentic Indian dishes, freshly made roti bread and local fruit juices. Breakfast is also available. While the food is a highlight, quick service isn't their strong suit.

Tu's Place

Martintar Street; tel: 672 2110; https://tusplace.webs.com; daily 7am–10.30pm; $$$

A lovely family-run joint that puts great emphasis on using locally sourced ingredients to create locally inspired dishes. In short, this is a great place to try something uniquely Fijian without having to travel too far from the main tourist drag. There are indeed other influences on the menu too, including Thai, Italian and Cajun-style foods. Since opening in 2005 this spot has remained perennially popular in Nadi.

Tiko's Floating Restaurant

Pacific Harbour

The Waters Edge Bar and Grill

Shop 86, Arts Village, Pacific Harbour; tel: 345 0145; www.thewatersedgefiji.com; Fri–Sun 10.30am–9pm, Tue–Thu 10.30am–5pm; $$

The beautiful deck-based seating at this water-facing feeding station is a great spot to see the big ball of fire in the sky dip into the sea of an evening, with a cocktail or cold beer in hand. Chase that down with something special from the menu, such as the snapper or the shrimp salad – both recommended.

Suva

Daikoku Suva

Shop 11, Dolphins Plaza, Victoria Parade; tel: 330 8968; www.daikokufiji.com; Mon–Sat noon–2pm and 6pm–10pm; $$$

The Suva sister restaurant to the Asian eatery that has taken Nadi by storm. Fantastic modern Japanese fare (sashimi, teppanyaki, sukiyaki, shabu shabu and so on) served with aplomb.

Downtown Boulevard

Ellery Street; daily 8am–6pm; $

If you're looking for a bite but just want to get something on the hop, without sitting down and waiting for service, hit this shopping centre food mall, where you can pick up delicious tucker from a range of cuisines, including Fijian fish and Indian curry dishes, but also pizzas and Chinese food.

The Galley

Royal Suva Yacht Club, Walu Bay; tel: 356 0682; Mon 10am–9pm, Tue–Sun 9am–9pm; $$

Overlooking the marina, this modest place punches above its weight with a mixture of Fijian fare (try the slowed-cooked beef soup – 'sui') and sensational seafood such as the seared tuna, all prepared by the popular chef, Rafa. Good views of the sunset are topped off with cold beers from the bar fridge. Prices are reasonable, and there's regular live music.

Governor's Museum Themed Restaurant

46–50 Knolly Street, Suva; tel: 337 5050; www.governorsfiji.com; Mon–Fri 9am–2.30pm, Sat from 8am, Sun 8am–2pm, Thu and Fri 6–10pm; $$$

With its hearty breakfasts (think eggs benedict and fritatas, awesome omelettes, creamy mushroom on toast or even NZ steak & eggs, all washed down with tropical fruits and good coffee) through to generous lunches (big burgers, monster sandwiches and daily South Seas specials), this centrally located joint has been massively popular since it opened a couple of years ago – and little surprise. In the evening, you can pair plates of fantastic food (ocean-fresh fish dishes, stuffed crab backs, giant sea prawns,

Have an Indian feast at Maya Dhaba

NZ lamb, char grilled steaks and great vegetarian dishes) with live music – all in a cracking colonial-design ambience.

The Great Wok

Corner of Bau Street & Laucala Bay Road; tel: 330 1285; daily 10.30am–11pm; $$

Sichuan food, well prepared and served in pleasant surroundings. There's a new renovated deck and a bar for pre-food beers. When you come to order, try the tokwat baby (pork and tofu with chili and vinegar sauce) or the special sizzling pork, served on a piping hot plate.

Maya Dhaba

281 Victoria Parade; tel 331 0045; Mon–Sat 11am–10pm; $$$

A reliable Indian option, which dishes up huge banquets and a range of classic dishes – lamb rogan josh, butter chicken and so on – through to an interesting goat curry. There's a decent wine list (a bit of a rarity in Fiji), although the atmosphere can be somewhat lacking.

Tiko's Floating Restaurant

Stinson Parade; tel: 331 3626; Mon–Fri noon–2pm, 6–10pm, Sat 6–10pm only; $$$

Although it's a restaurant on water, things won't feel too tipsy, as the former cruise boat is moored off Stinson Parade in calm Suva harbour, right in the CBD and just an easy walk from all the central hotels. You'll find a good range of seafood, as you would expect, plus plenty of beef and chicken dishes – vegetarians are not quite so well catered for.

Sigatoka and surrounds

Beach Cocomo Cafe

Queens Highway, Lot 1, Navoto Sovi Bay, Sigatoka; tel: 650 7333; dinner from 7pm (phone to reserve by 10am); $$

Call ahead to book at this boutique beachside place – which also offers bure accommodation – where just three tables sit pretty within a bamboo structure. Food is cooked to order (no menu) by chef Mary and you can't go wrong with the fish. Bring your own wine to complete the fine dining experience.

Flying Fin Restaurant n' Bar

Sunset Strip, Korotogo; daily 5–9pm; $$

The top pick from the menu here has to be the great local fish, but there are plenty of Western options too – from pizza and parmigiana through to onion rings, which keep kids happy – but, if you're really hungry, have a crack at the Bula Burger Challenge (it's massive – finish it and you'll score a free beer). The cocktails are good too, but it's the sunset view that really sells this place. After dark, films are sometimes shown. Free pick-up from some resorts, including Outrigger.

A fabulous beach picnic on Turtle Island

Shiva's Wine & Dine

Duabale Road, Sigatoka; tel: 995 6063; Mon, Tue and Sat 8am–5pm, Wed–Fri until 9pm; $$

Located near Sigatoka town square up some stairs that are not the easiest to find, Shiva's is the town's hidden secret. The menu includes filling fried rice dishes, curries as well as excellent Fijian classics; this is a good spot to try the kokoda, served in a coconut. An additional bonus is that this spot is air-conditioned. Nearby, Shiva's also has a Pizza Inn (Mon–Sat 8am–6pm), which sells a variety of fast foods, if you are looking to eat something a bit more familiar and less healthy.

Levuka

Kims Paak Kum Loong

Beach Street; tel: 344 0059; Mon–Sat 9am–3pm and 5–9pm; $

Beyond Whale's Tale (see page 60) there aren't too many places to eat in Levuka, but if you want somewhere that sells cold beer, you could do worse than this place, where traditional Chinese fare (plus the odd Thai and Fijian dish) is served for lunch and dinner in a setting that boasts a covered balcony eating area overlooking the main street. The breakfasts are also recommended.

Lautoka

Blue Ginger Café & Bar

Elizabeth Square, Opposite ANZ bank

Narara Parade; tel: 907 6553; Mon–Sat 8am–6.30pm; $

This brightly painted and friendly little place in Fiji's second largest city is a top spot for a great coffee (the real deal), a juice, smoothie or milkshake. Breakfasts and lunches are tasty, healthy and well-priced, and there's Wi-Fi.

Fins Restaurant

Marine Drive; tel: 666 4777; daily 6.30am–midnight; $$$

For a more upmarket option, nicely located on the waterfront, this restaurant is part of the Tanoa Waterfront Hotel. For simple breakfasts and lunches you might do better exploring other local options, but for a more substantial evening meal, the location and menu (which offers a range of surf and turf options, from fish to steak, plus burgers and pizzas) here offers something more substantial – and it's open on Sunday.

Savusavu

Arun's Taste of Hidden Paradise Restaurant

LTA building, Lesiaceva Road; tel: 937 2534; Mon–Sat 9am–9pm, Sun until 5pm; $

Found at the far end of Savusavu (towards the jetty), this joint offers really top-quality Indian food cooked fresh – entirely from scratch in fact – while you wait (occasionally for quite some time, depending on how busy

Crab and coconut make for a tasty South Pacific dish

they are). Just relax and enjoy your BYO beer/wine, as the results are well worth the wait. If you are in too much of a rush to order from the menu, buffet food is often available.

The Captain's Café
Copra Shed Marina; tel: 885 0511; daily 8am–9pm; $
With a great rotating menu that features pizza, sandwiches, burgers and other lovely lunch staples, this relaxing place also offers good breakfasts and does a cracking curry for a main meal. Staff are friendly, and the view from the deck, overlooking Savusavu bay, is sensational. It also opens on Sundays, when many other places in Savusavu are shut.

Savusavu Wok
Main Street; tel: 885 3688; daily 11am–9pm; $
Good Chinese food at really reasonable prices, served with a genuine smile. Despite a slightly tatty exterior, all the classic dishes are on offer here, like dumplings, crab, prawns and other seafood. Portions are generous. Cold beers and fruity bubbles of various flavours are available.

Taveuni

Coconut Grove Restaurant
Matei; tel: 888 0328; www. coconutgrovefiji.com; 8am–late; $$$
The menu at this spectacularly positioned restaurant (attached to accommodation) features traditional Fijian food and Indian-influenced options, all fantastic and freshly cooked. Book ahead if you're intending to come for dinner. Fijian-style entertainment is sometimes provided.

An imaginatively crafted dessert

Indulge in a cocktail at your resort

NIGHTLIFE

What constitutes nightlife in Fiji will very much depend on whereabouts in the country you find yourself. In the islands, where most visitors will probably spend the majority of their time, evening entertainment can consist of anything, including coconut bowling, hermit crab racing, croon-along sessions with local guitarists, toe tapping to cover bands, *bula* dancing lessons and sweaty sessions in backpacker discos.

Even the most basic of island resorts will have a bar, and they generally have someone working as the chief entertainment officer/party starter, who will get you up and dancing. **Beachcomber**, of course, has a reputation for being Fiji's party island, and in the midst of the season – mid November through January and February, when the island attracts a young crowd drawn from all over the world – decent DJs get things going, but don't go expecting Ayia Napa.

In the larger cities of Viti Levu, it's a slightly different story, and you can socialise with locals as well as other travellers. Even in Suva, there isn't the density of bars, clubs and live music joints that you might expect in the capital cities of larger, less scattered countries, but there are a few places well worth checking out. Don't hang around the streets after coming out of clubs – Fiji is a friendly place, but incidents do

still happen. Various venues feature live music one or two evenings a week, and local bands often have a reggae sound, which suits the tropical vibe.

Nadi

Ed's Bar

Kennedy Street, Martintar, Nadi; tel: 672 4650; Sun–Thu 5pm–2am, Fri–Sat until 5am
This popular party place has been around for coming up to three decades, but it's not showing any signs of calming down and getting sensible yet. Some come here for dance nights, glow parties and the sort of evenings that begin with beers and end in Jägerbombs. It's populated by a young up-for-it crowd, comprised of both locals and travellers. There's a garden and pool tables too.

Ice Bar

RB Jetpoint Complex, Queens Road, Martintar, Nadi; tel: 672 7144; www.facebook.com/icebar.fj; daily 3pm–5am
There's plenty of action at this stylish place, where you can choose between cutting a rug on the dance floor or sipping a cold beer on the balcony. The drinks are reasonably priced and there are pool tables too. It stays open later than anywhere else in town, but – and here's the really nice touch – the bar operates a shuttle bus to all the nearby resorts, to ensure visiting punters get home safe and sound.

Cloud 9's unique location

Suva

O'Reilly's

Corner of McArthur Street and Victoria Street, Suva; tel: 331 2884; open daily 7pm–3am

The heaving heart of Suva, O'Reilly's has been a popular party spot for years. It all starts off relatively sensibly, with pizza, pool and games of rugby on the screens, but the later you stay the looser it gets, as locals and visitors clink glasses of social lubricant in all its various forms. Bad Dog Café is attached to this joint so you can avoid drinking on empty.

Traps Bar

Victoria Parade, Suva; tel: 331 2922; open late

A classic bar-cum-club, Traps attracts a lively bunch of young locals, students and inquisitive visitors, and once they're in, the staff generally don't struggle to keep them entertained in the main bar which is normally bouncing with bodies well before midnight. There are several bar areas in this place, and it's worth looking out for live music, which often happens on Thursdays.

Savusavu

The Planters Club

Next to the LTA building, by the wharf; Mon–Sat 10am–10pm, Sun 10am–8pm

Savusavu isn't exactly known as a party place, but if cuddling a cold drink in a colonial setting sounds like a top night to you – and let's face it, there are worse ways to spend an afternoon and see the sun go down – then this joint is a good bet. Back in the day, this was a watering hole for planters to come and quench their thirst after bringing copra to market, and it's still a locals' hang out – ask one of them (or a member of the friendly staff) to sign you in. They put on a Sunday lunch *lovo* once a month. Happy hour lasts from 5.30– 6.30pm and you can order a meal from the Taste of Hidden Paradise Restaurant next door to enjoy with your beer.

Islands

Cloud 9

Vanua Malolo on Ro Ro Reef; tel: 869 7947; www.cloud9.com.fj; 10am–late

This place might be a bit bright for committed nightowls, but if you're going to settle into a tropical session, you may as well do it on a pontoon perched out in the azure waters of the South Pacific, under the Fijian sun, surrounded by coral reefs. There are various ways of getting out to Cloud 9 from Denarau, including aboard a jet boat called *Excitor* (www.excitorfiji. com). Once you've climbed aboard Cloud 9 there's a fully stocked bar with various international beers and top shelf drinks, as well as all the local favourites such as Fiji Gold, Fiji Bitter and Fiji Rum. The bar staff will whip up a tropical cocktail for you, and smoothies and bottled water are also available – because, of course, alcohol and water sports (which are also on offer) do not mix, so save your partying until you've dried off for the day. At weekends, international and local DJs really get the party going.

Firewalk entertainment at Shangri-La's Fijian Resort

A–Z

A

Age restrictions

People need to be at least 18 to drink alcohol or buy tobacco products in Fiji, and the age of consent is 16, irrespective of gender or sexual orientation.

B

Budgeting

Average costs for a range of items are listed below:
Bottle of Fiji Bitter: F$4.50
Bottle of drinkable wine (Australian reds and New Zealand whites are recommended): F$35–40
Street snack (eg roti): F$2-4
Meal at a curry restaurant: F$20
Main course at an expensive restaurant: F$50+
Cheap hotel: F$50–150
Moderate hotel: F$150–500
Deluxe hotel or resort: F$500
Taxi to the airport: F$15–20
Single bus ticket: F$1.50
Locally made Bula shirt: F$40
Sarong: F$20

Business hours

Business hours are (loosely) Monday–Friday 9am–5pm; Saturday 10am–1pm; assume most things will be closed on Sunday. There is a 24-hour bank service at the Nadi International Airport. Most shops and commercial outlets are open five days a week as well as on Saturday mornings.

C

Children

Fijians famously love children and you could not choose a better place to travel with kids. You may want to warn your infants in advance that people are quite likely to pick them up, squeeze their cheeks, tickle and cuddle them completely out of the blue. It's generally very easy to arrange baby sitting in resorts and lodges on the islands, and children are welcome most places – with the exception of some of the swankier resorts, which sometimes have a 16+ age restriction. Many islands have calm lagoons, which are safe for toddlers and young children to paddle around in (carefully supervised, obviously) and perfect for teaching kids to snorkel.

Clothing

Visitors to Fiji need a light tropical wardrobe: swimwear, shorts, T-shirts and, as you'll quickly discover, *sulus* (known also throughout the Pacific as *parea* or sarongs), are a must for both men and women. There are at least 10 different ways in which women can use it, even

Fiji's calm waters are perfect for children

for evening wear. As the largest Christian denomination in Fiji is Wesleyan (Methodist), visitors are asked to be careful not to offend local sensibilities. Wearing bikinis and ultra-brief trunks is fine at resorts but definitely not when visiting villages or shopping in town. At such times it is easy to take a *sulu* to use as a wraparound so that no offence is caused. Wearing a hat in a village can also cause offence.

Consulates and embassies

Australian High Commission: 37 Princes Road, Tamavua, Suva; tel: 338 2211; www.fiji.embassy.gov.au
British Consulate: Victoria House, 47 Gladstone Road, Suva; tel: 322 9100; www.gov.uk
Canadian Consulate: 6 Cawa Road, Martintar, Nadi; tel: 992 4999; www.canadainternational.gc.ca
New Zealand High Commission: 8th Floor, Reserve Bank of Fiji Building, Pratt St, Suva; tel: 331 1422
South African High Commission: Plot 1, 16 Kimberly Street, Corner Gordon Street, Suva; tel: 331 1087
US Embassy: 158 Princes Road, Tamavua, Suva; tel: 331 4466; https://fj.usembassy.gov

Crime and safety

Common-sense rules apply when visiting Fiji – the country has a very low rate of crime against visitors but it makes sense to be careful. It is advisable not to wander about alone in any of the urban areas late at night or in the early hours of the morning, especially when worse for wear because of drink. There have been cases of muggings, but these are rare. Women should also avoid going to secluded beaches alone. A problem that you're more likely to encounter are 'sword-sellers' and 'guides' who trade on the gullibility of visitors (see page 21).

Customs

After collecting their luggage, visitors will find two signs: NOTHING TO DECLARE and GOODS TO DECLARE. Those with nothing to declare will quickly find their way to the concourse outside the hall. If you're bringing tobacco or alcohol in, normal passenger allowances apply. Check your allowances (www.frcs.org.fj/arriving-in-fiji) if you're in doubt.

Disabled travellers

Local attitudes towards mobility impairment are positive: people will help out wherever possible, but it's rare to find modified access to many places, and it can be particularly hard to visit popular places such as the Mamanuca and Yasawa Islands, where ferries don't dock, instead dropping passengers off into smaller boats. For this reason, it may be better to fly to Mana island. The Fiji Disabled Peoples Association (FNCDP Complex, 3 Brown Street, Toorak Suva; tel: 331 1203; www.pacificdisability.org) can offer more detailed advice.

Sevusevu ceremony

E

Electricity

The electrical current in Fiji is 240 volts AC 50Hz. Fiji has generally three-pin power outlets identical to those in Australia and New Zealand. If your appliances are HOV, check for a 110/240V switch; if there is none, you will need a voltage converter. Leading hotels and resorts generally offer universal outlets for 240V or 110V shavers and hairdryers and so on.

Emergencies

In an emergency – for police, fire or ambulance – call 911.

Other locally useful numbers include the following:

Nadi ambulance, tel: 6701128; hospital, tel: 6701128; police, tel: 6700222. Urgent pharmacy, Westside Drugs open Sunday 10am-noon and thereafter on call, tel: 6700310, 6780188, 6780044.

Suva ambulance, tel: 3301439; hospital, tel: 3313444; police, tel: 3311222. Check with the hospital for the nearest rostered urgent pharmacy.

Lautoka ambulance, tel: 6660399; hospital, tel: 6660399; police, tel: 6660222.

Etiquette

When visiting traditional villages, wear modest attire (nothing too skimpy) and remove any headwear (including caps). Don't touch people on the head. Be respectful to the village chief (and everyone else, but especially the chief!). When visiting villages independently, bring a gift (*yaqona* is ideal – you can get it at markets).

F

Festivals and holidays

Fiji observes a range of Christian, Hindu and Muslim holidays, and celebrates significant historical events – see Festivals (see page 28) for more details.

In addition to the variable dates for Easter and Good Friday (April/May), Diwali (October/November) and Prophet Mohammed's Birthday, the following are public holidays:

1 January – New Year's Day
7 September – Constitution Day
10 October – Fiji Day
25 December – Christmas Day
26 December – Boxing Day

H

Health

Healthcare and insurance

Fiji is free of major tropical diseases, including malaria. It has an effective, Western-style medical system, although local people still believe in age-old herbal remedies. The government is encouraging an awareness of the importance of diet and hygiene to health, and supports the municipalities in the provision of safe drinking water.

Fresh water in Suva, Lautoka and the other major towns is treated and is generally safe to drink from the tap. This applies to hotels and resorts but not at remote villages. Some resorts use artesian water for bathing, but provide drinking water separately. If so, visitors will be advised.

Hospitals are located in the major centres, and there are health centres in rural areas. Hotels and resorts usually have a qualified nurse on the premises and a doctor on call. It is wise to take out a comprehensive health insurance.

Inoculations

A Yellow fever and cholera vaccinations are only required if coming from an infected area. Hepatitis A and B jabs are advised.

Pharmacies

There are reasonably well-stocked pharmacies in major towns and cities, but bring any essential medication with you. It is rare to find a pharmacy that is open 24/7; check with the nearest hospital first – see emergencies.

I

Internet

Access to the internet is available in most parts of Fiji. In addition to sites at all major hotels, internet cafés are abundant in major cities and towns.

L

LGBTQ+ travellers

Although homosexuality has been traditionally frowned upon by local laws and religious leaders, in 1997, Fiji became only the second country in the world to explicitly protect against discrimination based on sexual orientation in its constitution. Overly physical public displays of affection are not recommended, but this applies to heterosexual couples too.

Left luggage

Most hotels in Nadi will store your luggage for you if your flight out is later in the day.

M

Media

The *Fiji Times* and the *Fiji Sun* are the two surviving daily newspapers.

Radio

The government, through the Fiji Broadcasting Commission, operates Radio Fiji in AM and FM frequencies: English (1089AM and 104FM); Hindi (774AM and 98FM); and Fijian, (558AM). Broadcast times begin at 5pm and continue until midnight. Radio Navtarang is an independent station operating on FM96 24 hours a day.

Television

Fiji TV is the leading television broadcaster in Fiji and the Pacific region,

Underwater life in Fiji's waters

operating the most-watched free-to-air TV stations in the country, including Fiji One, EMTV and SKY Pacific, the Pacific's premium satellite pay TV service.

Money

The Fijian dollar is the basic unit of currency – notes are available in denominations of $5, $10, $20, $50 and $100, while coins are issued in 5c, 10c, 20c, 50c, $1 and $2.

F$1 is worth £0.36, US$0.47, AU$0.65, NZ$0.69 and €0.41 at time of writing. Up-to-date exchange rates against all the major currencies are posted each day in all banks, listed in newspapers and displayed at most hotels. There is no limit on the amount of money brought in. Visitors are allowed to take out currency up to the amount imported.

Cash machines

You will find Automatic Teller Machines (ATMs) at the airport upon arrival, and in the major cities of Nadi and Suva, where Australian banks such as ANZ and Westpac have a presence. However, do not reply on access to an ATM anywhere else in the country.

Credit cards

American Express, Visa and Master-Card are all readily accepted, with Diners Club less popular. Some restaurants and companies levy a credit-card charge, usually around 2 or 3 percent. Major credit cards are welcomed by most hotels, restaurants, shops, rental car agencies, tours, cruises and travel agents. American Express, Diners Club, Visa, JCB International and MasterCard are represented in Suva.

Taxes

In 2016, Fiji dropped its VAT rate from 15 percent to 9 percent. However, there was an increase in the Service Turnover Tax (STT, which is levied on hotel accommodation, restaurants and cafes, cinemas, car hire and tour operators) from 5 percent to 10 percent at the same time, and a 6 percent Environment Levy was also introduced. For visitors, this means that as of 1 January 2016, they are paying 25 percent tax on top of their hotel rates (this is comprised of: 9 percent VAT, 10 percent Service Turnover Tax and 6 percent Environment Levy). This is often now absorbed into the price you will be quoted, but it is always best to check before committing to a booking.

Tipping

Tipping is not encouraged in Fiji and it is left to the individual to determine whether or not to pay a gratuity. Though tipping is not a local custom, you will find local people tipping. This has much to do with social attitudes as it is a recognition of good service. Fijians ritually exchange gifts of food, clothing, *yaqona*, tabu, kerosene and even money during important social occasions.

A starry night on Turtle Island

P

Police

In an emergency, dial 911
Police should be immediately contacted in all cases of crime, and also for visa extensions when away from Suva, Nadi, Lautoka and Levuka. Local numbers are:
Labasa tel: 8881222
Lautoka tel: 6660222
Levuka tel: 3440222
Nadi tel: 6700222
Nausori tel: 3477222
Navua tel: 3460222
Rakiraki tel: 6694222
Savusavu tel: 8850222
Sigatoka tel: 6500222
Suva tel: 3311222
Taveuni tel: 8880222

Post

Post offices open 8am–4pm, Monday to Friday, at all the main centres. Letters addressed to c/o The Post Office at the designated area will be held for you and delivered on proof of identity. Telegram, fax and telephone services are also available.

R

Religion

The majority of indigenous Fijians are practising Christians (mostly Methodist); there is also a large Hindu population and a significant Muslim population.

S

Smoking

Fiji has strict no-smoking laws, and sparking up in public places (including bars, nightclubs, restaurants and retail outlets) can earn you a steep fine.

T

Telephones

The country code for Fiji is 679. There are no area codes on the islands, so to call Fiji from outside the country, dial your international access code followed by 679 and the number you require. Many hotels and resorts have direct dialling facilities (IDD), and card phones are available in many shops and stores. Look for the Telecom call card signage on display.

Mobile (cell) phones

Fiji is well serviced by local mobile networks including Vodafone Fiji, Digicel and Inkk Mobile. You can also arrange roaming status before travelling here as well as on arrival. The country system is GSM 900, which is the same as Australia and New Zealand, but many North American phones – which are CDMA-band only – will not work in Fiji.

Time zones

Fiji is 12 hours ahead of GMT. So, when it is 9am in Fiji, it is (depending on whether daylight saving alterations have been made in other countries):

London: 9pm the previous day
Frankfurt: 10pm the previous day
New York: 4pm the previous day
Los Angeles: 1pm the previous day
Tokyo: 6am the same day
Sydney: 7am the same day
Auckland: 9am the same day

Toilets

There are some public toilets in larger cities, but it's best to make use of hotel and better restaurant facilities when possible.

Tourist information

Tourism Fiji (www.fiji.travel) is the official organisation that provides advice and guidance for all visitors to the 'Home of Happiness'. Their head office is found in Nadi (Suite 107, Colonial Plaza, Namaka, Nadi; tel: 672 2433).

Tours and guides

The Tourism Fiji website (www.fiji.travel) is an excellent resource for finding a reputable guide for any area and/or activity that you might be interested in.

Transport

Arrival

Virtually everyone will arrive in Fiji by air, flying into Nadi international airport, where they will be greeted by someone in a Bula shirt playing the guitar. Taxis into town from the airport to your accommodation should cost around F$15–20. If you are arriving independently by boat, you will need to clear customs in Suva, Lautoka, Levuka or Savusavu.

Getting around

Buses

Fiji is a small country and it's cheap to travel by local transport. Bus companies offer express and normal services. With the express service, it is possible to go from Lautoka to Suva with stops only at Nadi, Sigatoka and Navua as well as at the hotels. Normal bus services will pick up and let off passengers where they find them. Carrier services usually operate within a confined area. Your hotel tour desk will advise. Otherwise, contact **Pacific Transport** (tel: 330 4366; www.pacifictransport.com.fj) or **Sunbeam Transport** (tel: 338 2122; www.sunbeamfiji.com). Tour companies offer more luxurious buses – with comfortable seats and air-conditioning – at a higher price. Check with your hotel tour desk.

Driving

Rental cars are not cheap in Fiji, due in part to the extremely high rate of import duty levied by the government on vehicles. Rental car companies are obliged to recover a good deal of the cost of the new vehicle within a 2-year operating period before selling the car. As in all things, it pays in the long run to stick with brand names such as Avis (tel: 6722233; www.avis.com) and Hertz (tel: 672 3466; www.hertz.com).

Drivers require a valid license from an English-speaking country, or an International Driving license.

Hazards when you're on the road include drivers who overtake at blind corners, or who stop abruptly on the road without pulling to the side, and horses and cattle which, unrestrained by fences, wander as and where they please.

Ferries

There are several major domestic shipping lines which carry passengers between islands, including **Goundar Shipping** (Suva to Savusavu, Taveuni; Koro; tel: 330 1035) and **Fiji Searoad Service** (running from Suva to the islands of Ovalau and Vanua Levu; tel: 344 0125; www.fijisearoad.com).

For ferries around the Mamanuca and Yasawa Islands, contact **Awesome Adventures Fiji** (tel: 675 0499; www.awesomefiji.com) and **South Sea Cruises** (tel: 675 0500; www.ssc.com.fj).

Flights

Fiji Airways (tel: 672 0888; www.fijiairways.com) fly from Nadi International and Suva to regional airports including Cicia, Kadavu, Koro, Labasa, Lakeba, Rotuma, Savusavu, Suva, Taveuni and Vanuabalavu.

Taxis

There is a profusion of taxis and there is none of the frustration of some other parts of the world when a taxi is never available when you want it. In Fiji, they come looking for you, and they're cheap. Each taxi is required by law to have a meter but many do not turn it on. Insist that the driver turns the meter on when you begin the ride, and if he refuses to comply, step out of the cab.

Drivers will also happily make 'deals' for sightseeing and excursions for the day.

Visas and passports

A passport valid for at least 3 months beyond the intended period of stay and a ticket for onward travel is required, as well as sufficient funds for your visit. Tourist visas are granted on arrival, free of charge, for a stay of up to 30 days for citizens of Commonwealth countries and nationals of most countries. Consult the Department of Immigration (www.immigration.gov.fj) if in doubt, or if you wish to work or stay more than 6 months.

Websites

Tourism Fiji's website is your best first port of call for any questions you might have about visiting Fiji: www.fiji.travel.

Women

Fiji is generally a safe country for all travellers, including women travelling in groups or alone – but common sense and caution should always be applied, particularly late at night in urban areas, and when under the influence of alcohol.

Weights and measures

Fiji uses the metric system of weights, measures and temperatures.

Bula! A resort welcome ceremony

LANGUAGE

Fiji has three official languages: English, Fijian and Hindi. Due to its history, the lingua franca of the country is English, although both the indigenous population and large Indo-Fijian community commonly converse in their own languages. The version of Hindi spoken in Fiji is sometimes called Fiji Hindi, because it has evolved into a distinct dialect. Hotel staff are always fluent in English.

Historically, Fijian was exclusively an oral language and there are actually around 300 different dialects that fall under the general term Fijian – although fortunately for foreigners who wish to make an attempt to try the native tongue (an effort that will be warmly appreciated), there is one standard form of the language that is understood right across the islands.

The Wesleyan missionaries who first reduced the Fijian language to a written form were faced with a number of sounds peculiar to the language. For example, a Fijian will never pronounce the letter 'd' as in day. In the Fijian language, the 'd' sound is always preceded by 'n' so that it will be pronounced 'nd' as in Nandi (which is how Nadi, as in the city, is actually pronounced). This also applies to the letter 'b' which becomes 'mb', This is always confusing to visitors who will invariably keep mispronouncing many words such as Sigatoka, which is actually pronounced as Singatoka, Beqa, which is Bengga and the Mamanuca Islands when it should be pronounced as the Mamanutha Islands.

No wonder people are confused. The following should be of help. The vowels are pronounced as in the continental languages. The unusual consonant sounds are accounted thus:

B is 'mb' as in 'remember'
C is 'th' as in 'them'
D is 'nd' as in 'candy'
J is 'ch' as in 'church'
G is 'ng' as in 'singalong'
Q is 'g' as in 'great'

Useful phrases

Politeness is a highly valued quality across all the islands of Fiji, and making an effort to express your gratitude for hos pitality, or respectfully indicating your preference for one thing over another, in Fijian will win you plenty of friends.

Hello *Ni Sa Bula*
Hello! (informal) *Bula!*
Hello (formal, when addressing a chief) *Ni Sa Bula Vinaka Saka*
No *Sega*
No thanks *Sega Vinaka*
Fine, thank you *Sa Bula Bula Vinaka Tiko*
How are you? (informal) *Sa vakacava tiko?*

Building a bilibili

How are you? (formal) *Bulabula vinaka o'kemuni?*
Pardon? *Ō?*
Please *Kerekere*
Sorry *Vosoti au*
Thank you *Vinaka*
Thank you very much *Vinaka vaka levu*
Yes *Io* (pronounced 'Ee-yo')

BOOKS AND FILM

Many visitors arrive in Fiji with their heads full of preconceived images formed after viewing films such as *The Blue Lagoon* and TV series like *Survivor: Fiji* – but the country has far deeper and more complex stories to tell.

Prior to the arrival of Europeans, however, indigenous Fijians – like many of the cultures scattered across the islands of the South Pacific – had no written tradition. Tales involving historical events, folklore and legend – including creation myths – were passed on orally, and storytelling formed an important part of *kava* ceremonies (as it still does).

The written word was a powerful tool for missionaries as they attempted – very successfully – to convert the population of the islands to Christianity, but the emphasis was all about teaching the population to read (the Bible), not to express themselves with the pen.

It wasn't until Fiji gained independence from Britain in 1970 that the country really began developing its own distinct voice in the literary and (later still) cinematic sense. The University of the South Pacific had been established two years earlier, with its major campus in Suva, and this soon began to act as a catalyst for creativity, with the founding of the South Pacific Arts Society and the launching of art-and-literature journal *Mana*.

Books

Raymond Pillai was a pioneer of Indo-Fijian literature and is heralded as one of Fiji's greatest creative talents. His first collection of short stories, *The Celebration*, wasn't published until 1980, but an earlier poem called 'Labourer's Lament' (published in 1974) prophetically dealt with a future Fiji where racism and coups play a large role. One of Pillai's plays, *Adhura Sapna* (begun in 1977 but not published until 2001) is regarded as the first work of literature voiced in Fiji Hindi. It also explores the complicated relationship between the country's Indian and Fijian communities.

Another writer who has articulated the Fiji-Indian experience is Subramani, author of *The Fantasy Eaters: Stories From Fiji*, published in 1988. The book, which is comprised of nine short stories and a novella, tells a series of tales about Fiji's immigrant population and their descendants, and explores how traditions the community have brought with them from India interplay with modern life in the South Pacific.

Other recommended writers include the politician and author Satendra Nandan (*The Wounded Sea, Requiem for a Rainbow, Fiji: Paradise in Pieces*), Indo-Fijian poet Sudesh Mishra; playwright and director Larry Thomas, author of *The Anniversary Present*, whose characters are renowned for giving a voice to

Francis Rossi and Rick Parfitt in Bula Quo!

some of Fiji's most marginalised people; and the contemporary novelist Joseph Veramu, whose novels include *Moving Through the Streets* and various other children's stories.

Film

Unsurprisingly, given its eye-candy qualities, Fiji has starred in numerous films over the years. In 1932, Douglas Fairbanks Snr appeared in *Mr Robinson Crusoe*, filmed in Fiji, Samoa and Tahiti. The first version of *The Blue Lagoon*, starring Jean Simmons, was shot on Sawailau in the Yasawas in 1949, and Burt Lancaster starred in *His Majesty O'Keefe* in 1953, with filming locations including Pacific Harbour and Suva.

The 1979 remake of *The Blue Lagoon*, featuring Brooke Shields and Leo McKern, was filmed on Nanuya Levu, Yasawa, and a third incarnation, *Return to the Blue Lagoon* (1992), starring Milla Jovovich and Brian Krause, was shot in Taveuni. Tommy Lee Jones appeared in *Savage Island* in 1983, with scenes shot in Pacific Harbour.

Cast Away, starring Tom Hanks and a volleyball called Wilson, came out in 2000 – showing Monuriki Island in the Mamanucas in a gorgeous, if remote, light.

From this high point, 2013's *Bula Quo!* (aka Guitars, Guns & Paradise) offers something really different – a film featuring Francis Rossi and Rick Parfitt from the band Status Quo, playing themselves in an action comedy that sees them witness a gang murder and outwit the local mafia to foil an organ-smuggling racket during a concert tour of Fiji. Yes, really.

The local film industry is still somewhat embryonic. The inaugural Islands in the World International Film Festival (IWOIFF) was hosted by the University of the South Pacific in Suva, in April 2013 precisely because, as writer and director Larry Thomas put it: 'There have been many films made about the Pacific but hardly any from the point of view of Pacific Islanders themselves.'

However, several noted Fijian writers have also written and directed works for the big and small screen. In 2007, for example, after several years of the Fiji-Indian diaspora that started after the 2000 coup, Raymond Pillai's play *Adhura Sapna* was adapted and turned into a film.

As an author, Vilsoni Hereniko received the Elliott Cades Writing Award for his contribution to literature (for works including the plays *Don't Cry Mama, A Child For Iva, Sera's Choice* and *The Monster*), but he's now known more as a film director.

Hereniko wrote and directed Fiji's first and most famous feature film, *The Land Has Eyes* (Pear ta ma 'on maf). The film, set in Hereniko's native Rotuma, is a coming-of-age story starring Sapeta Taito. It screened at the Sundance Film Festival in 2004, was Fiji's official submission to the 2006 Academy Awards, and collected the 'Best Overall Entry' award at the 2005 Wairoa Maori Film Festival, and the 'Best Dramatic Feature' award at the 2004 Toronto ImagineNATIVE Film & Media Arts Festival.

ABOUT THIS BOOK

This *Explore Guide* has been produced by the editors of Insight Guides, whose books have set the standard for visual travel guides since 1970. With top-quality photography and authoritative recommendations, these guidebooks bring you the very best routes and itineraries in the world's most exciting destinations.

BEST ROUTES

The routes in the book provide something to suit all budgets, tastes and trip lengths. As well as covering the destination's many classic attractions, the itineraries track lesser-known sights. The routes embrace a range of interests, so whether you are an art fan, a gourmet, a history buff or have kids to entertain, you will find an option to suit.

We recommend reading the whole of a route before setting out. This should help you to familiarise yourself with it and enable you to plan where to stop for refreshments – options are shown in the 'Food and Drink' box at the end of each tour.

For our pick of the tours by theme, consult Recommended Routes for... (see pages 6–7).

INTRODUCTION

The routes are set in context by this introductory section, giving an overview of the destination to set the scene, plus background information on food and drink, shopping and more, while a succinct history timeline highlights the key events over the centuries.

DIRECTORY

Also supporting the routes is a Directory chapter, with a clearly organised A–Z of practical information, our pick of where to stay while you are there and select restaurant listings; these eateries complement the more low-key cafés and restaurants that feature within the routes and are intended to offer a wider choice for evening dining. Also included here are some nightlife listings, plus a handy language guide and our recommendations for books and films about the destination.

ABOUT THE AUTHORS

This book was written by Patrick Kinsella, a freelance journalist and editor originally from the busy and built-up streets of southeast England – which goes a long way to explaining why he enjoys exploring the beautiful beaches, tropical islands and dizzying highlands of far-flung Fiji quite as much as he does. A dual citizen of the United Kingdom and Australia, Patrick has also worked on Insight Guides Explore Sydney, Melbourne, Queensland and New Zealand.

CONTACT THE EDITORS

We hope you find this Explore Guide useful, interesting and a pleasure to read. If you have any questions or feedback on the text, pictures or maps, please do let us know. If you have noticed any errors or outdated facts, or have suggestions for places to include on the routes, we would be delighted to hear from you. Please drop us an email at hello@insightguides.com. Thanks!

CREDITS

Explore Fiji
Editor: Sian Marsh
Author: Patrick Kinsella
Head of DTP and Pre-Press: Rebeka Davies
Updated By: Paul Stafford
Managing Editor: Carine Tracanelli
Picture Editor: Tom Smyth
Cartography: original cartography
Berndtson & Berndtson, updated by Carte
Photo credits: Alamy 6BC, 7MR, 12/13,
18, 18/19, 19L, 20, 29, 42, 43, 47, 48,
49, 52, 52/53, 54, 56/57, 58, 59, 60, 87;
Anais Chaine Photography 38, 40; AWL
Images 4/5T; Beqa Lagoon Resort 4MC, 7T,
8MC, 24/25, 63, 96; Captain Cook Cruises
6ML, 8MC, 12, 94, 100; Chris McLennan/
Jean-Michel Cousteau Fiji Resort 4ML, 4MC,
10, 11, 74MC, 82, 101; Chris McLennan/
Starwood Hotels & Resorts 36MC, 84; Corbis
62; Daikoku 85; DoubleTree 74/75T, 77;
Getty Images 1, 7M, 13L, 14/15, 21, 23,
24, 26, 30/31, 32, 33, 36/37T, 44/45, 46,
50, 51, 53L, 57L, 61, 68, 69, 70, 86; iStock
7MR; Jean-Michel Cousteau Fiji Resort 4MR,
8ML, 22, 36MR, 83; Leonardo 4MR, 8MR,
16, 16/17, 17L, 25L, 36MR, 39L, 38/39,
71, 74MR, 74MR, 76, 78, 89B, 90, 93, 95,
98, 99; Matt Frost/REX/Shutterstock 103;
Moviestore/REX/Shutterstock 102; Robert
Harding 8/9T, 34/35, 64/65; Shangri-La
Hotels & Resorts 4ML, 8ML, 27, 36MC,
74ML, 74MC, 79, 92; Shutterstock 6MC, 28,
41, 55, 56; Toberua Island Resort 80, 81;
Tor Johnson/TOR Photograph 72/73, 74ML,
91; Turtle Island 6TL, 8MR, 36ML, 36ML, 66,
66/67, 67L, 88, 89T, 97
Cover credits: AWL Images (main) iStock
(bottom)

Printed by CTPS – China
All Rights Reserved
© 2019 Apa Digital (CH) AG and
Apa Publications (UK) Ltd

Second Edition 2019

DISTRIBUTION

UK, Ireland and Europe
Apa Publications (UK) Ltd
sales@insightguides.com
United States and Canada
Ingram Publisher Services
ips@ingramcontent.com
Australia and New Zealand
Woodslane
info@woodslane.com.au
Southeast Asia
Apa Publications (Singapore) Pte
singaporeoffice@insightguides.com
Worldwide
Apa Publications (UK) Ltd
sales@insightguides.com

SPECIAL SALES, CONTENT LICENSING AND COPUBLISHING

Insight Guides can be purchased in bulk
quantities at discounted prices. We can
create special editions, personalised jackets
and corporate imprints tailored to your needs.
sales@insightguides.com
www.insightguides.biz

INDEX

MAP LEGEND

- ● Start of tour
- → Tour & route direction
- ❶ Recommended sight
- ❷ Recommended restaurant/café
- ★ Place of interest
- ❶ Tourist information
- ✈ International Airport
- ✈ Airport/Airfield
- ✉ Post office
- Ⅰ Statue/monument
- Ⅿ Museum/gallery
- 📖 Library
- 🎭 Theatre
- ⊕ Hospital
- ✿ Police
- ✝ Church
- 🚌 Main bus station
- 🏖 Beach
- Lighthouse
- Scuba diving
- Deep sea fishing
- 2713 Altitude in m
- Important building
- Urban area
- Park
- Non-urban area

INSIGHT ⊙ GUIDES
OFF THE SHELF

Since 1970, INSIGHT GUIDES has provided a unique perspective on the world's best travel destinations by using specially commissioned photography and illuminating text written by local authors.

Whether you're planning a city break, a walking tour or the journey of a lifetime, our superb range of guidebooks and phrasebooks will inspire you to discover more about your chosen destination.

INSIGHT GUIDES

offer a unique combination of stunning photos, absorbing narrative and detailed maps, providing all the inspiration and information you need.

PHRASEBOOKS & DICTIONARIES

help users to feel at home, when away. Pocket-sized with a free app to download, they go where you do.

CITY GUIDES

pack hundreds of great photos into a smaller format with detailed practical information, so you can navigate the world's top cities with confidence.

EXPLORE GUIDES

feature easy-to-follow walks and itineraries in the world's most exciting destinations, with our choice of the best places to eat and drink along the way.

POCKET GUIDES

combine concise information on where to go and what to do in a handy compact format, ideal on the ground. Includes a full-colour, fold-out map.

EXPERIENCE GUIDES

feature offbeat perspectives and secret gems for experienced travellers, with a collection of over 100 ideas for a memorable stay in a city.

www.insightguides.com